vatch's thai street food

vatch's thai street food
vatcharin bhumichitr

photography by Martin Brigdale
and Somchai Phongphaisarnkit

kyle books

for my brother, ed

This edition pubilshed in 2007 by Kyle Books
An imprint of Kyle Cathie Limited
www.kylecathie.com

Distributed by National Book Network
4501 Forbes Boulevard, Suite 200
Lanham, MD 20706
(301) 459 3366

ISBN (13-digit) 978 1 904920 60 1

Design and Art Direction Geoff Hayes
Food Photography Martin Brigdale
Travel Photography Somchai Phongphaisarnkit
Project Editor Sheila Davies
Copy Editor Catherine Ward
Stylist Helen Trent
Home economists Linda Tubby
Production Sha Huxtable & Alice Holloway

Vatcharin Bhumichitr is hereby identified as the author of this work in
accordance with Section 77 of the Copyright, Designs and Patents
Act 1988.

Bhumichitr, Vatcharin
Vatch's Thai Street Food/Vatcharin Bhumichitr.
1. Cookery, Thailand
A Library of Congress Number is available on request

Color reproduction by Sang Choy International
Printed in Singapore by Star Standard

1 3 5 7 9 8 6 4 2

**Woman selling sweetcorn
in front of the giant
chedi, Nakhon Pathom.**

contents

introduction   06

bangkok   30

around bangkok   50

by the sea   72

the north   94

the northeast   116

index   144

Anytime, Anywhere, and Cheap

We heard them before we saw them, each with their unique sound. All manner of noises: the bong of a hand bell or the ping of a bicycle bell, the chock of wood striking a worn block, the clack of something like Spanish castanets, or, the most obvious, the clang of a spoon against a pan. As greedy children, we knew what, or rather whom, each noise represented, so we were ready for the spectacle that eventually ambled along our soi, the Thai word for the lanes that run off the thanom, or main city arteries. And what a spectacle it was as each vendor pulled, pushed, or pedaled his customized storage box or cooking range past our house. The most common and simple was the hahp, a bamboo shoulder pole with rattan frames at each end holding baskets, evenly balanced so the vendor could pass down narrow alleyways, or travel on the little boats from up-country villages, into the city early every morning. Some just brought fruit and vegetables straight from their farms, while others came with ready-prepared dishes or the wherewithal to cook them. You could often see a slim young lady or a wizened old grandmother kneeling on the ground beside her hahp, but if you tried to lift it you'd be surprised at how heavy it was—they could carry amazing weights. You still see them everywhere: by the river or crossing busy city intersections. They

Woman selling grilled sausages and other north eastern specialities at the night food market, Surin.

are the moving restaurants of Asia, and are so important there is even a proverb about them: "a broken hahp is like a broken home." Another common spectacle in our soi was the pushcart or tricycle cart, a simple variant of the bicycle pushing a large wheeled box containing everything needed to make delicious food.

We children didn't care how the food arrived—we just wanted lots of it, so when we heard the bell or the block, we would rush out and order noodles or sweets or ice cream before our mothers could stop us. We knew what many tourists have learned since, that this was the most convenient, the freshest, and cheapest food available.

If you want a street vendor, you'll find clusters of them at any market, bus or train terminal, or near busy city office blocks. There are also special food areas in all the major city centers—anyone will tell you where. The food is great because vendors specialize in one dish, often grow their own ingredients, or get them fresh from that day's market and use classic country recipes—which is the point of this book. These are the basic recipes of Thai cuisine, which, because they have to be made on the move, are usually very easy to cook.

We children loved the street food sellers and, by the time our mothers caught up with us, the cooking would be started and they would have to pay. Naturally, this would annoy them very much but there was nothing they could do. Until, that is, the arrival of See Ooey. This gruesome character came from China and, starting in the south of Thailand, worked his way north, kidnapping and murdering children on the way. He would wait down a quiet lane for the food vendors to pass and then pounce. Horrible as it was, it was a gift for our mothers who would call "See Ooey will get you if you go out," which stopped us for a while. I don't know the full story, but the tale was even embellished with threats that See Ooey ate his victims. Eventually they caught him near Rayong on the coast east of Bangkok. He confessed and was condemned to death without any problem. There is a grisly souvenir of those days in the Siriraj Hospital, where his remains are pickled and on display. I understand that tourists can visit them in some sort of ghoulish

A typical *hahp* food seller, the most common form of street food selling in Thailand.

ghoulish tour. At the time, it only interfered with our eating habits, though it meant more to my youngest brother who is also called Ooey and so, was given a hard time at school by the other boys.

Street food really is the lifeline of Asia, helping feed millions of people daily. The first European tourists, the backpackers, hanging around Kow San Road (the street featured in the film, *The Beach*) discovered it was a cheap and delicious way to eat. They soon turned Kow San Road into a food market and open-air restaurant, and began the process of popularizing Thai food, which has now spread around the world. Curiously enough, today the whole business is reversed, with Bangkokians going to eat in Kow San Road because the food is good and they get a free cabaret, staring at the crazy antics of the young foreigners.

Street food is always on the move, not just down narrow lanes but also in entire urban areas. In the rapidly expanding cities of Asia, with their ever-shifting centers of activity, from banking to tourism, it is the ability of street vendors to speedily adapt to changes that makes them so essential to the well-being of millions of people. When I was young, the streets around Pratunam (the Watergate), near to what was then Bangkok's main modern shopping area, were lined with food sellers, not only during store hours but also at night, when young people would meet up after a show or a club or just to enjoy a bowl of noodles in the cooler night air. Many a love affair began on the tiny stools clustered around Pratunam's food stalls. Today, things have moved on. There are newer, more exciting, shopping centers, and all that remains at the once-famous Pratunam, is the seafood market opposite the Amari Watergate Hotel.

By contrast, a totally new food area sprang up when the Bangkok Bank opened its new headquarters on Silom (Windmill) Road. No doubt many of the vendors from Pratunam also moved to what is now one of the city's largest open-air restaurants, clustered at the foot of the bank's building, serving not only the clerks and managers from the bank, but the hundreds of workers in what has become the hub of the city's financial district. One can see different examples of this adaptability around the country.

Because of the oppressive heat in Surin, a major town in the once isolated northeastern province of Isan, street food sellers have turned night into day.

Street food becomes a restaurant in the night food market, Surin.

To most tourists, Surin is only on the map because of the famous large-scale annual elephant roundup, or the elephant training village at nearby Ban Ta Klang, but Surin is worth a visit to see the equally large-scale night market. A typical trader is a woman I spoke to, who was making the famous Isan spicy salad Som Tam, which is now made throughout Thailand. She turns up at 9 P.M. and is bent over her large stone mortar, pounding grated papaya, nuts, and chilies, well into the night. Her regular spot is on the Thanon Krung Sri Nai, a long street in the town center, which has the regular town market for fruit, vegetables, and spices at one end, and what is effectively a huge open-air restaurant of street food sellers at the other. Because of the heat, the market suppliers deliver during the night, and the shoppers come at dawn. The food sellers feed the traders during the dark hours, the shoppers at dawn, and even provide light suppers for late-night diners. They cluster in groups, offering a range of dishes, and transform themselves into restaurants with small tables and stools. Children will run and get beers and sodas from nearby stores. The whole place is brightly lit with colored neon strips, and buzzing with excitement. I last visited during the rainy season and it was like a swimming pool, but still fascinating. A typical customer is Khun Patcharin, the brother of a friend of mine in England, who cultivates oyster mushrooms and delivers them to the market at 2 A.M. He then chooses his food seller and has his main meal of the day. Actually, he is surrounded by street food—his farm is near a famous scenic area, the town's main reservoir, which attracts people by its fresher air and is where street sellers come to provide instant picnics. This is a key point, that in Thailand you don't need a street to have street food. You can find it anywhere—on beaches and by rivers and highways, on railway station platforms as well as in the train carriages.

Street sellers are very ingenious. They know, for example, that most drivers leave Bangkok around 8 A.M., so they cluster at the point where the average driver will be on any road at about noon, ready for lunch. This is particularly noticeable as you drive across the invisible provincial border into Isan itself, where you suddenly start to see large model chickens by the roadside, which indicate that there are food vendors selling the famous Gai Yang barbecued chicken. Every place has its local specialities. On popular beaches on the Gulf Coast west of Bangkok, like those at Cha-am and Hua Hin, food sellers with their hahps or trays ceaselessly parade with seafood and shellfish, or gather in clusters making open-air beach restaurants, where squid and shrimp are grilled, and mussels steamed. Thais expect to find special food everywhere, and an impromptu picnic is often the main reason for visiting somewhere.

One of the biggest food areas in the country is in a town not far from Bangkok called Nakhon Pathom, renowned for its giant chedi or bell-shaped temple, which is one of the largest Buddhist monuments in the world and certainly the largest in Thailand. All the streets around it are full of food stalls, and at its base is a vast open-air restaurant, which is as much street theater as food supplier—vendors toss balls of ice cream in the air and catch them in cones for enchanted children; cake sellers display sweets in every color of the rainbow. It really doesn't have very much to do with pure Buddhism, which counsels restraint in everything, but to see such excess is certainly worth a day out.

Because they are such convenient one-dish meals, you find many street food vendors selling the same dishes all over Thailand. Nevertheless, I've divided this book into the five main food areas of the country because some important differences still remain. While it is true that food vendors congregating in and around the capital have given Bangkok and its surrounding region the most varied menu in the country, it is also the most strongly influenced by Chinese cuisine. Regionally, the greatest differences come from the influence of neighboring countries, and the use of local ingredients—Malaysia and seafood in the south, Burma and rich sauces in the north, Laos and plentiful charcuterie in the northeast. There is a straight split between the center and the south, where conventional paddy rice is the staple, and the north and northeast, where sticky or glutinous rice is preferred. You'll find all these differences reflected in this book.

One of the traditional places to find street food is along the rivers and klongs, the canals that crisscross the country. Worth a visit is the former capital, Ayutthaya, a city of canals with sensational ruins and monuments. Here you will find many fine floating restaurants as well as traditional Gueyteow Rua, or noodle boats, which still pass up and down its waterways. I like to go to Ayutthaya's Patuchai area, where they sell Roti Si Mi (silk threads), a pancake stuffed with sweet noodles that look like fine hair— hence the name. I don't give the recipe because it's far too complicated, but it's well worth walking along the street in Ayutthaya to see the noodle makers tease out the ball of wheat flour, sugar, and water into fine threads so quickly they seem like magicians. Extraordinarily, they are all Muslims who at some point traveled from the south looking for work. I talked to Bang Somboom Arun, who does a sort of roadside show with his son who is learning the trade. Bang Somboon's brother traveled first to Bangkok, where he eventually settled and met a Vietnamese woman who taught him to make the threads, a Vietnamese speciality. He didn't have a shop, so he walked the streets selling the filled pancakes out of two brass tins carried on his back like two cookie tins, with open windows set in them so people could see what he was offering. Bang Somboon joined him and took over the business while his brother went on to make Kow Mok Gai, a Muslim chicken dish. Bang Somboon is just one of a large Muslim community in Ayutthaya, proof of how street food unites the country. He still has his brother's brass tins, but he has settled down on a fixed site now, where people come to him.

Many of the street sellers are poor people who want to make a living for themselves, a widow, perhaps, who is left without any resources except her ability to cook, or a young man with limited education. They start by carrying

The author buying a palm fruit beside the freeway from Bangkok to Petchaburi.

their hahps around, progress to a pushcart, then hope to find a fixed spot with other food sellers and eventually grow to a roadside restaurant, employing other people. Thailand abounds with stories of people who have made it rich this way. My brother, Ed, was eating at a stall in Yaowarat, Bangkok's Chinatown, famous for its food, when he heard one of the boys who were serving say to his brother: "Mother's tired now, go and get the Mercedes." He pointed to the Chinese woman who was cooking at a steaming pot in the corner. Sure enough, it wasn't a joke. A Mercedes duly appeared and they started packing up. She had made her money, but was too superstitious to break her luck by giving up what had brought her good fortune. Near to the Grand Palace in Bangkok, a woman called Khun Pa Ni Chiapchalaart used to sell Khao Niew Manuang (Sticky Rice with Mango). She now has a famous shop selling the best sweet rice and succulent mangoes, and people make pilgrimages to buy them.

Food vendors come into their own at special occasions, particularly temple celebrations and village fairs. Two of the biggest are not yet on the regular tourist circuit, but well worth a visit. The village of Ban Ta Klang, near Surin in northeastern Thailand, is famous for training elephants. It's full of them, and they wander around free and friendly. In fact, the village is often referred to simply as Moo Bahn Chang (elephant village). It's near the border with Cambodia and most of the people, who speak Khmer, treat the elephants as part of the family—they show respect to them like they do to grandfathers and grandmothers, because they have such long lives. In April or May, just before the rains come, the men finish studying or farming and spend a short time in the local temple as novice monks. At the monk-making ceremony, the men's heads are shaved, they are dressed in white, and made up in bright colors, and carried to the temple in an enormous procession of brightly caparisoned elephants that wends its way from the

river Mae Nam Wang Ta. Look through the village to the monastery and you will find long lines of food stalls, which have been set up to feed the hundreds of visitors who come to see the great spectacle. The elephants often help themselves to tidbits as they amble along.

It's the same in Chiang Mai at about the same time, when they hold the Inthakhin Festival. The Inthakhin Pillar, which is kept at Wat Chedi Luang, is not really a simple pillar, but a phallic fertility symbol, a survivor of the old animist beliefs that preceded Buddhism. It is sacred to most northerners who come to pray for abundant rains and a plentiful harvest at the May/June festival. Thousands of people take part in the week-long festival. Young boys in ancient military uniforms parade around, and the food is very special, with the vendors dressing up in historical costumes trying to sell authentic food from the past.

It would be wrong to imagine that with modern urban life, street food will disappear. While it is true that the new shopping malls and department stores attract many city customers with their giant food halls, these places actually use the same principle as the street food open-air restaurants, and effectively, it is street food moved indoors. Both are simply lines of individual cooks, each specializing in one particular dish. Street food really is the best type of cuisine, and I have been gathering these recipes on the lanes, highways, rivers, and beaches of Thailand since I was that greedy little boy. My favorite meal is still when I find a crowded market in a new place, pick a street vendor, and eat something local that I haven't tried before. I hope this book helps you share some of my experiences.

Bang Somboon Arun making 'silk threads' (*Roti Si Mi*).

before you begin

Equipment

The average Western kitchen should have all the equipment necessary for these recipes, although it would be an advantage to have a large mortar and pestle. You will also need a steamer (see page 29).

Amounts

The quantities given for each dish (unless otherwise stated) will provide enough for a light snack for two people if eaten on its own, or enough for four if part of a larger meal with other dishes.

Ingredients

1 Thai cooks do not go by measurements but by flavor, so you should always sample everything and adjust the amounts I have given to suit your personal taste. The quantities here could be thought of as average, but more or less of anything, chilies or fish sauce for example, can be used if needed.

2 It is also best to remember that vegetables in Asia tend to be smaller than those in Europe or America, so try not to select giant bulbous specimens when shopping for these ingredients. Chili and garlic always have a more intense flavor in Asia than in the West so you may find you'd like to adjust their quantities accordingly.

3 As a general principle, everything should be cut into bite-sized pieces (as we seldom use knives at the table), and always under- rather than over-cook.

4 Even canned goods tend to vary, particularly coconut milk, which can be thicker or thinner depending on the brand. As I cannot list every supplier here, it is a good idea to try a few varieties and choose your own individual favorites.

5 With fish, it is important to know that Thais like to deep-fry the whole fish until it is quite hard, then eat everything including any little bones. I have given Thai cooking times, but if you like your fish more moist, and with the bones removed, you will need to adjust the cooking time accordingly.

6 Overall, you must remember that a Thai cook works more by intuition than by measurement, and you should follow this system to some extent when cooking Thai food for yourself. If it tastes good, go with it.

Holy basil.

fresh ingredients

Banana leaf

Although not really a cooking ingredient, banana leaves are often used in Thailand to serve food on, and to wrap up and enclose food before steaming or grilling. Cooking food in banana leaves gives it a slight but distinctive flavor, but if you can't get hold of them, tin foil is an adequate substitute. Bamboo and lotus leaves are also used in this way but are probably even harder to get hold of in the West.

Basil

Sweet basil (bai horabha), the variety most commonly found in Europe and America, has shiny green leaves tinged with purple, and a smell tinged with cinnamon and cloves. It is cooked at the last minute or used fresh as a garnish. Holy or Thai basil (bai krapow) has narrower, slightly hairy leaves, a stronger taste, and it must be cooked.

Chili

Three varieties are used in this book: small red or green chilies (prik khee noo), about an inch long and fiery; medium red or green chilies (prik chee faa), finger-length, about three inches long, and less hot; and large dried red chilies (prik haeng), about three inches long, and medium hot.

Chinese celery (kunchai)

This is similar to Western celery, but has looser stems, smaller diameter, and a much stronger flavor, which means some adjustment if you substitute another variety. Choose those with the fattest and whitest stalks, since these will be the most tender. Chop them more finely than you would with Western celery, since they can be stringy.

Pea eggplants and the larger hard green eggplants.

Young ginger.

Coriander/cilantro (pak chee)

Closely resembling Italian or flat-leaf parsley, cilantro (fresh coriander leaves) are used as a garnish. Coriander root and/or stalk is usually crushed to make a paste, or chopped and added as a cooking ingredient. Roots and stalks can be frozen.

Eggplant

Four varieties of eggplant are used in southeast Asian cuisine, two soft and two hard. The soft eggplants are the large purple/black eggplant, familiar in the West; and the long, thin, pink-skinned eggplant. The hard ones include the small, round, green eggplant, about an inch in diameter, and the pea eggplant, also green and rather like an inflated garden pea. These last two will only be available in specialty Asian markets.

Galangal (khaa)

This creamy-white rhizome is slightly harder than ginger (see below). It is used in the same way, but has a more lemony flavor.

Ginger (king)

Knobbly, golden-beige "fingers" of fresh ginger are now readily available from supermarkets, but are often old or musty. Try to buy the young roots (rhizomes), which are pinker in color. Well-wrapped, fresh ginger can be kept for up to two weeks in a refrigerator. It also freezes well and can be grated from frozen.

Kaffir lime, see lime

Lemon grass (takrai)

This widely used herb is sold as long, lemon-scented blades, always with the leaves chopped off. Try to buy pale-green, almost white, bulbous stalks, roughly nine inches long. If they are old, you will need to peel away the hard outer leaves down to the tender center. When cooked, lemon grass imparts a fresh citrus taste with a touch of ginger, but without the bitter acidity of lemon or lime. Rings of chopped lemon grass can be frozen and used directly from the freezer.

Lime (manao)

Little green limes are the most common citrus flavoring in southeast Asian cooking. Lemons can be substituted in a pinch. Where kaffir lime (bai magrut) is specified, it is usually the lime leaves that are needed, which add tang, or the skin or zest, which has a strong citrus punch. To shred lime leaves, pile them on top of one another, then roll them into a "cigarette," and cut them across in very thin slices to produce fine slivers of leaf.

Long bean (tua ffak yow)

At up to a yard in length, the aptly named long bean resembles a wildly overgrown string bean (which can be used as a substitute). The long bean, however, is crunchier and cooks faster. Choose darker beans with small bean seeds inside the pods.

Mooli, see white radish

Morning glory/ water spinach (pak boong)

With a slight flavor of Western spinach, the long jointed stems of this water vegetable remain firm when cooked, while the arrow-shaped leaves quickly go limp. The leaves will turn yellow and go off if not used promptly.

Mushroom

Dried fungus mushrooms (cloud ears) are the most common Asian mushroom. They are usually black, but there is a white variety. Both are easily available and are usually bought in 2-ounce packages. They should be soaked at room temperature until soft (20–30 minutes), then checked to see that no sandy grit remains. The smaller they are, the better. Readily available Western varieties, which you can use instead, include the champignon or white mushroom, the large flat parasol mushroom, and the straw mushroom, which is slightly more pointed than the white mushroom, as well as the oyster or pleurotte mushroom.

"Lesser" garlic (krachai)

A long, thin rhizome has a slightly lemony, gingery flavor. It should be peeled, and is prepared in the same way as ginger. Available from Asian markets.

Papaya/pawpaw (malako)

This large, green, gourd-like fruit, with soft yellow-orange flesh, is eaten like melon. When unripe and still green, the hard flesh is grated and used as a vegetable.

Taro (pooak)

This large oval tuber, which needs to be peeled, is cooked in the same way as potato. It can be found in Chinese or Indian specialty stores.

Turmeric (khamin)

Brown and flaky on the outside, bright orange-yellow inside, this rhizome adds a warm, spicy taste, but is mostly used dried and ground, to add color. Fresh turmeric is now more widely available in the West, but only buy small amounts. Treat fresh turmeric like ginger: cut off a small section, peel it, then chop or pound it according to the instructions in the recipe.

Water spinach, see morning glory

White radish (mooli)

This long, white, root vegetable, with a cool sharpness when raw, is a bit like turnip when cooked. It can also be found in Japanese stores, where it is known as daikon.

Bamboo shoot.

the pantry

Bamboo shoots (normai)

The "shoot" is the first soft stage of the bamboo when it appears out of the ground, before it hardens into the cane. The shoot has to be stripped of its needle-sharp hairs, and boiled to remove the bitter, poisonous acid. Don't worry, though, even in Asia bamboo shoots are bought ready-prepared by experts, and in the West they are always bought canned. They can be divided into "spring" shoots and "winter" shoots, the latter being considered the more tender and sweet. Unfortunately, the cans seldom indicate which variety they contain. Canned in brine, they are yellowish in color and, after opening, may be kept in water in a sealed container in a refrigerator for several days.

Bean curd sheets (*fong tao hou*)

These are sold dried in packets. They are quite fragile but will separate easily if soaked for 5–6 minutes. Torn sections can be patched with other sheets

Bean sauce (tow jiew)

This is made from mashed and fermented soybeans—black or yellow. Black bean sauce is thick with a rich flavor; yellow bean sauce is more salty and pungent. Black bean sauce is most commonly used.

Chili oil

One method of making chili oil involves first broiling dried chilies with fresh garlic and shallots, then pounding them to a paste, and stir-frying in oil to give a powerful, hot flavor. Another method involves frying the dried chilies, garlic, and shallots, in oil until crisp, then pounding and stir-frying. You can make chili oil yourself (see page 26), but many people prefer to buy it ready-made in bottles. Each country has its own version and there is little differ-ence between them. You will only need quite small amounts, but it will keep, well-sealed, in a refrigerator for at least a year.

Chili powder (prik pon)

This red powder, made by grinding small dried red chilies, is sold in jars, cans, packages, or cardboard boxes. .

Coconut milk or cream

Buy this in cans. The thin liquid that collects at the top of the can (before it is shaken or stirred) is called coconut milk. After stirring or shaking, the thick liquid is called coconut cream. It's as simple as that!

Dried shrimp (gung haeng)

These tiny sun-dried shrimp, sold loose or in jars or plastic bags, will keep for a long time. They are not meant to be reconstituted by soaking in water, but are used as flavoring. Choose those that are not too pink or salty. See shrimp paste.

Fish ball (louchin pla) **and Fish cake**

The fish and flour dumplings and the fish cake can be bought ready-made from Chinese stores. They are already cooked, and simply need reheating.

Fish sauce (nam pla)

The "salt" of southeast Asia, this liquid—extracted from fermented fish—is the principal savory taste in nearly all the recipes in this book. The best fish sauce is young, with a light whiskey color and a refreshingly salty taste; the worst is old, dark, and bitter. The easiest to find are those from Thailand (nam pla) or Vietnam (nuoc mam). The amount of fish sauce in a dish is clearly a matter of taste. I have prescribed modest quantities, so taste, and add more if you wish. Strict vegetarians, who do not eat fish, should substitute light soy sauce, bearing in mind that it is less salty so more will be needed.

Jasmine flower water

This can be bought ready-made, or you can make it yourself by soaking ten jasmine flowers in two cups of water for about an hour.

Lotus seeds

These preserved seeds are available from Asian markets.

Moong/Mung beans

These small, yellow, dried beans are often used in desserts and need to be presoaked to soften them. Available from Asian markets .

Oil

As a general rule, southeast Asian cooking demands a neutral-flavored vegetable oil both for cooking and as an ingredient. In Thailand, oil used to be made by frying pig fat over a low heat. This is now considered to be very unhealthy and most Thais now use plain vegetable oil. Flavors are added by frying garlic or shallots in the oil at the beginning of the cooking process. There are occasional exceptions: some Chinese-based dishes need sesame oil for its rich flavor; other dishes come from territories that produce a particularly flavorful nut oil (generally peanut), which colors the dish. Uniquely for Asia, the Filipinos, under the heavy influence of Spain, have taken to using olive oil for some of their dishes, especially salads. For all other countries in the region, however, olive, and other distinctively-flavored oils, should be strictly avoided.

Palm sugar/jaggery (nam tan peep)

This is made from the sap of the coconut palm. It is sold in compressed cakes that keep well. The best is soft and brown and has a rich toffee-like aroma. Usually used in desserts, it is an essential ingredient if you want the full caramel taste of some southeast Asian dishes. Dark turbinado sugar is a possible, but poor, substitute. Available from Asian markets.

Pickled cabbage (pak gat dong)

Small pieces of firm white cabbage preserved in boiled vinegar, salt, and sugar, for at least three days. It is served as a relish, or cooked and added, as a salty slightly-sour ingredient, to a variety of dishes.

Pickled garlic (kratium dong)

Normally this is bought ready-prepared in a jar, but you can make it yourself · if you wish. Soak a pound of whole garlic cloves (unpeeled) in a bowl of cold water for one hour, then drain, and pull away the skins. Let the cloves dry for an hour. In the meantime, heat a cup of rice vinegar in a heavy saucepan, and add one cup of sugar and two tablespoons of salt. Dissolve over a low heat, then let cool. Place the garlic in a preserving jar, pour the cold liquid over it, close tightly, and leave for at least one month before using.

Pork ball (louchin moo)

This is a pork and flour dumpling, bought ready-made in Chinese stores.

Preserved plum (bue dong)

This is sold preserved in syrup in Asian markets and is used to make sweet plum sauce.

Preserved radish, turnip, or other vegetable

Chi po is preserved white radish or mooli, and tang chi is made from a variety of hard vegetable stems, most often cabbage. In both cases, the vegetable is mashed with salt and allowed to "sweat." After several repeats and a sun-drying process, the preserved vegetables are packed into sealed jars or plastic bags, and sold in Asian markets. Only small slivers are needed to enhance the flavor of a dish.

Shrimp paste (kapee)

This dark purple paste has a formidable smell that disappears on cooking, and adds a rich pungent taste to any dish. Store in a tightly-sealed jar or risk a malodorous kitchen. See dried shrimp.

Soy sauce (siew)

This is made from soybeans. Light soy sauce is light-colored, almost clear, with a delicately salty taste. Dark soy sauce is thicker and stronger, and used mainly to add color to a dish.

Spring roll wrappers

These paper-thin dough wrappers can be bought ready-made in packages, often frozen.

Tamarind (makham)

The pulp extracted from the pods of the tamarind tree is used to impart a pungent, sour, lemony flavor. Buy it in compressed blocks. Most recipes call for it to be dissolved in water to make "tamarind water" or "tamarind liquid." Place a lump of tamarind, roughly equivalent to a heaped tablespoon, in warm water and knead it until the water is deep brown and all the flavor has been extracted.

Tofu (bean curd)

Tofu is often sold in 4-ounce cakes, with a little milky liquid. It is best used on the day of purchase, but may be kept for up to three days in a refrigerator, provided the liquid is poured away each day and replaced with fresh water. Cubes of deep-fried tofu, or bean curd, are usually available in Asian markets, but deep-frying your own fresh tofu until it is golden brown produces something so superior that I strongly recommend making the extra effort.

Vinegar

While rice vinegar would be authentic, usually any plain, light, white wine vinegar can be substituted.

Wonton wrappers

These are available in pre-cut sheets from Asian markets. Unlike spring roll wrappers, which are white in color, these are yellow. Wonton wrappers are often sold vacuum-packed in the freezer section.

Water chestnuts

These small, sweet and juicy tubers add a crunchy texture to a dish. They are sold in cans in Asian markets and in many supermarkets.

Pickled garlic (left) and tamarind pods (right).

rice

Sticky or glutinous rice (khao niew)
Nearly always served with northern Thai or Lao food, this is a broad short-grain rice, usually white but sometimes brown or black. When cooked, it is thick and slightly porridgey in texture, and can be rolled into a ball and used as a scoop for other food. Sadly, it cannot be cooked in an electric rice-steamer.

To cook one pound of sticky rice, cover in water and soak for at least three hours, preferably overnight. Drain, and rinse thoroughly. Line the perforated part of a steamer with a double thickness of muslin or cheesecloth, and place the rice on top. Bring the water in the bottom of the steamer to a boil and steam the rice over medium heat for 30 minutes.

sweet sticky rice balls

Sticky rice is also used in desserts. In this recipe, the sticky rice is formed into balls and dipped in sugar syrup.

1³/₄ cups cooked sticky rice
3 cups granulated sugar
1¹/₂ cups water
food dyes (optional)

Divide the rice and dip it in different food dyes, as your fancy dictates. Place the sugar and water in a heavy saucepan and dissolve the sugar over low heat. Bring to a boil, and boil rapidly to form a thick syrup. Remove from the heat. Take small handfuls of the colored rice and form it into rice balls, then dip into the sugar syrup. Remove with a slotted spoon and place on a metal tray to harden.

noodles

There are five varieties of noodle commonly used in Thailand. You can buy most of these fresh in Asian markets, but it is more likely that you will find them dried. All dried noodles, with the exception of ba mee noodles, need to be soaked in cold water for about 20 minutes before cooking (wun sen noodles need slightly less time). The dry weight will usually double after soaking, thus four ounces dry noodles will produce about eight ounces soaked noodles. After soaking, they should be drained before cooking. To cook, dunk them in boiling water for 2–3 seconds, or stir-fry according to the recipe.

Sen yai

Sometimes called "rice river noodle" or "rice stick," this is a broad, flat, white, rice flour noodle. Usually bought fresh, when it is rather sticky and needs to be separated before cooking, but it can also be bought dried.

Sen mee

A small, wiry-looking, rice flour noodle, usually sold dried and sometimes called "rice vermicelli."

Sen lek

A medium-sized rice flour noodle, usually sold dried. The city of Chanthaburi is famous for sen lek noodles, which are sometimes called "Jantaboon noodles," after the nickname for the town.

Ba mee

An egg-and-rice-flour noodle, medium yellow in color, which comes in a variety of shapes, each with its own name. It is very unlikely that you will see anything other than the commonest form, which is thin and spaghetti-like, curled up in "nests" that need to be shaken loose before cooking.

Wun sen

A very thin, very wiry, translucent, soybean flour noodle, also called "vermicelli" or "cellophane" noodle. Only available dried.

the four flavors kruang prung

While each noodle dish has its own distinctive taste, the final flavor is left to the diner, who can adjust the taste by sprinkling on quite small amounts of the Four Flavors. These are always put out in little serving bowls whenever noodles are served. The flavors are:

1 Chilies in fish sauce (nam pla prik): 4 small fresh red or green chilies, finely chopped, in a 1/4-cup of fish sauce.

2 Chilies in rice vinegar (prink nam som): 4 small fresh red or green chilies, finely chopped, in a 1/4-cup of rice vinegar.

3 Sugar (nam tan)

4 Chili powder (prik pon)

prepared sauces

Curry and Chili Pastes

There are five curry or chili pastes used frequently in Thai cooking. Many can now be bought ready-made in Asian markets or even canned in Western supermarkets. If you would like to make your own, here are the recipes:

green curry paste gaeng kiow wan

2 long green chilies, chopped

10 small green chilies, chopped

2 tablespoons chopped lemon grass

4 shallots, chopped

2 tablespoons chopped garlic

1-inch piece galangal, chopped (see page 17)

1 teaspoon ground coriander seed

1 tablespoon chopped cilantro root

1 teaspoon chopped kaffir lime skin **or** finely chopped lime leaves

2 teaspoons shrimp paste (see page 21)

1/2 teaspoon ground cumin

1/2 teaspoon ground white pepper

1 teaspoon salt

Using a mortar and pestle, blend all the ingredients together to form a smooth paste.

red curry paste gaeng pet

8 dried long red chilies, seeded and chopped

1 teaspoon ground coriander seed

1/2 teaspoon ground cumin seed

1 teaspoon ground white pepper

2 tablespoons chopped garlic (about 4 cloves)

2 stalks lemon grass, finely chopped

3 cilantro roots, chopped

1 teaspoon chopped kaffir lime skin **or** finely chopped lime leaves

1-inch piece galangal, chopped (see page 17)

2 teaspoons shrimp paste (see page 21)

1 teaspoon salt

Using a mortar and pestle, blend all the ingredients to make a smooth paste. This recipe should make about a quarter-cup of paste.

dry curry paste panaeng

10 dried long red chilies, seeded and chopped

5 shallots, chopped

2 tablespoons chopped garlic (about 4 cloves)

2 stalks lemon grass, chopped

1-inch piece galangal, chopped (see page 17)

1 teaspoon ground coriander seed

1 teaspoon ground cumin

3 cilantro roots, chopped

1 teaspoon shrimp paste (see page 21)

2 tablespoons roasted peanuts

Using a mortar and pestle, blend all the ingredients together to form a smooth paste. This recipe should make about six tablespoons paste.

massaman paste massaman

10 dried long red chilies, seeded and chopped

1 tablespoon ground coriander seed

1 teaspoon ground cumin

1 teaspoon ground cinnamon

1 teaspoon ground cloves

1–2 star anise

1 teaspoon ground cardamom

1 teaspoon ground white pepper

1/4 cup chopped shallots (about 6 shallots)

1/4 cup chopped garlic (about 7 cloves)

about a 2-inch piece lemon grass, chopped

1/2-inch piece galangal, chopped (see page 17)

1 tablespoon chopped kaffir lime skin or finely chopped lime leaves

1 tablespoon shrimp paste (see page 21)

1 tablespoon salt

Blend the chilies, coriander seeds, cumin, cinnamon, cloves, star anise, cardamom, and white pepper together in a mortar and pestle. Add the rest of the ingredients, one by one, blending after each addition, until you have a smooth paste. This recipe should make about six tablespoons paste.

broiled chili oil

tom yam sauce (nam prik pao)

5 garlic cloves, peeled

5 shallots, peeled

5 long dried red chilies, seeded and chopped

1/4 cup vegetable oil

2 teaspoons sugar

1 teaspoon salt

1 tablespoon ground dried shrimp

1 Place the garlic, shallots, and dried red chilies on a piece of foil and place under a pre-heated broiler, turning occasionally with tongs, until the skins start to blister and become charred.

2 Using a mortar and pestle, pound together to make a paste.

3 In a small frying pan, heat the oil and add the paste. Stir a couple of times in the hot oil, then add the sugar, salt, and ground dried shrimp. Cook for 5 minutes, stirring all the time.

cooking techniques

Boiling meat

We have a way of cooking chicken or duck breast that ensures they are neither tough nor overcooked. Place the breast in a pan, just cover with cold water, bring to a boil, then remove from the heat. Cover with the pan lid and leave in the boiled water for 10 minutes, until just cooked through.

Crisp-frying

To add flavor and a crunchy texture to a dish, some ingredients—such as dried shrimp, chopped garlic and shallots, and shredded lime leaf—are fried in hot oil until they crisp up.

Dry-frying

Again to add flavor and a crunchy texture to a dish, ingredients like grated coconut, uncooked rice grains, sesame seeds (white or black), and sunflower seeds, are placed in a frying pan without oil and heated until they darken and release their aroma. Sesame seeds will jump around as they warm up.

Deep-frying

Spring rolls, banana fritters, and pork toasts are all deep-fried. It is easiest to use a deep-fat fryer, set to a temperature of 400°F., but you can also use a deep pot set over a high heat. Vegetable oil is generally used.

Grinding or powdering

Dry-fried ingredients can be ground to a powder in a mortar. This will impart the same flavor as the whole dry-fried ingredients, but will give the dish a different, smoother texture. Dried shrimp can also be ground to a fine white powder, but you can buy them ready-ground pre-packed.

Steaming

This method is used for cooking sticky rice and a number of other recipes. Either use a traditional Chinese bamboo steamer, or improvise with a large pot, using an upturned heatproof bowl in the bottom of it, to support a plate above the boiling water in the pot.

Stir-frying

This is always done very quickly over a very high heat. Oil is added to a hot wok and when it begins to form a haze, the ingredients are tossed in—garlic first, to flavor the oil, followed in turn by meat, noodles, sauce, and then vegetables. These are stirred and turned rapidly over a high heat until the hardest ingredients are just cooked and still crunchy. Stir-fries should be eaten immediately.

bangkok

Early travelers visiting Bangkok recorded how the Thais lived both beside the water and in it, so close was their relationship to the river and the interconnected network of canals that made up the city's main highways. These water dwellers, living in stilt houses half in and half out of the water, received all their supplies by boat, including their meals. Food sellers sailed in noodle boats (*rhua*), complete with a heater to boil the water for the noodles and a pan in which to cook the sauce; they can still be seen today on many canals that secretly exist behind the tall buildings. Water-borne street food is the original street food of Thailand, and most visitors catch a glimpse of it at the famous floating market on the outskirts of modern Bangkok.

thai fried noodles with shrimp pad thai gung

When I was young, one of the attractive things about street food was its availability. Take Pad Thai, which you could find anywhere day or night, depending on whether you were a well-off day worker or on one of the poorer night shifts. Cheaper versions would be cooked with just a little deep-fried tofu, and sprinkled with some ground dried shrimp to give it some flavor. The more you paid, the more meat or seafood you could request, or you could even get fresh shrimp. Today, the grander cooks wrap and serve it in a net of fried egg strands to customers waiting in Mercedes cars, but in its original adaptable state it was, for a time, virtually the national dish, found everywhere and served in one form or another to everyone.

2 tablespoons vegetable oil

2 garlic cloves, finely chopped

4 king or tiger shrimp, peeled and de-veined

1 large egg

6 ounces sen lek noodles (see page 24), soaked and drained

2 tablespoons lemon juice

1¹/₂ tablespoons fish sauce

¹/₂ teaspoon granulated sugar

2 tablespoons crushed roasted peanuts

2 tablespoons dried shrimp (see page 19), ground or pounded

¹/₂ teaspoon chili powder

1 tablespoon chopped preserved radish (chi po, see page 20)

¹/₂ cup fresh bean sprouts

2 scallions, cut into 1-inch lengths

for garnishing
a sprig of fresh cilantro, coarsely chopped
lemon wedges

1 In a wok or frying pan, heat the oil and fry the garlic until golden brown. Add the shrimp and stir well. Break in the egg and stir quickly, cooking for a couple of seconds.

2 Add the soaked noodles and stir well. Stir in the lemon juice, fish sauce, sugar, half the peanuts, half the dried shrimp, the chili powder, the preserved radish, 1 tablespoon of the bean sprouts, and the scallions. Keep stirring until the noodles are cooked through—about 3 minutes, then turn onto a serving dish.

3 Arrange the remaining peanuts, dried shrimp, and bean sprouts over the noodle mixture. To serve, place a little pile of chili powder, and another of sugar, on the side of the dish to be mixed in as each diner wishes. Garnish with fresh cilantro and lemon wedges.

chicken fried rice with basil leaves
khao pad krapow gai

This is one of those rare Thai dishes that has lost some of its original character on its journey from Thailand to the West. The basil leaves are included for their delicate flavor, and because they need very little cooking, we mince the meat so finely it's almost ground, in order to shorten the cooking time. In the West, however, because ground meat is looked down on, many restaurants tend to use larger slices of meat which results in the basil going limp from the longer cooking time. Decide for yourself—if you want an authentic taste, reduce the cooking time by grinding the meat or cutting it very very finely.

2 tablespoons vegetable oil

2 garlic cloves, finely chopped

2 small fresh red chilies, finely chopped

1 cup ground or very finely chopped chicken

1 tablespoon fish sauce

1/4 teaspoon granulated sugar

1 tablespoon light soy sauce

20 fresh holy basil leaves

13/4 cups boiled fragrant rice

1 small onion, slivered

1/2 red or green sweet pepper, finely chopped into thin matchsticks

1 In a wok or frying pan, heat the oil until a light haze appears. Add the garlic and fry until golden brown. Stir in the chilies and the chicken. Add the fish sauce, sugar, and soy sauce, and stir-fry over a high heat until the chicken is cooked through.

2 Toss in the basil leaves, followed by the cooked rice, and mix gently together. Add the onion and the sweet pepper, and stir quickly to mix. Turn onto a serving dish.

beef curry with sweet basil
penang nua

2 tablespoons vegetable oil

2 garlic cloves, finely chopped

1 tablespoon red curry paste (see page 25)

a 6-ounce tender beef steak, finely sliced

1/2 cup coconut cream

1 tablespoon crushed roasted peanuts

20 fresh sweet basil leaves

for garnishing

1 long fresh red chili, finely slivered lengthwise

2 kaffir lime leaves, rolled up into a cigarette shape, and finely slivered

1 In a wok or frying pan, heat the oil and fry the garlic until it begins to brown. Add the curry paste and stir in well.

2 Add the beef, coconut cream, crushed peanuts, and basil leaves, stirring well after each addition. Stir-fry over high heat until the beef is cooked through.

3 Turn onto a serving dish and garnish with the slivered chili and kaffir lime leaves.

pork belly with five spices moo pa low

Pork belly with five spices in the foreground and curried rice with chicken, food market, Bangkok.

Street vendors like to serve this dish because it can be prepared in advance and served over several days—unlike many Thai dishes that need to be made at the last minute. It is also thought to be a good, mild accompaniment to hot dishes like curries, so people who have bought the one will often buy this, too, as a counterbalance.

6 eggs

2 tablespoons vegetable oil

2 large garlic cloves, finely chopped

1 tablespoon finely chopped cilantro root

2 tablespoons five-spice powder

1¹/₂ pounds pork belly, cut into 1-inch pieces

5 cups chicken stock

2 tablespoons dark soy sauce

3 tablespoons fish sauce

2 tablespoons granulated sugar

for garnishing

a few fresh cilantro leaves

1 Hard-boil the eggs, let them cool, then peel and set aside.

2 In a large pot, heat the oil and fry the garlic until golden brown. Stirring constantly, add the cilantro root and then the five-spice powder.

3 Add the pork and stir-fry over high heat until the meat is thoroughly coated with the spices, and cooked through. Pour in the stock and bring to a boil. Stir in the soy sauce, fish sauce, and sugar, then add the hard-boiled eggs. Reduce the heat and simmer gently for 30 minutes, skimming off any scum as it forms.

4 Pour into a serving bowl, garnish with fresh cilantro leaves, and serve.

pork fried with ginger and pineapple moo pad king sapparot

5 large dried black fungus mushrooms (see page 17), soaked in cold
 water for 10 minutes
2 tablespoons vegetable oil
2 garlic cloves, finely chopped
an 8-ounce piece pork tenderloin, thinly sliced into strips
1 medium onion, roughly chopped
a heaped cup pineapple chunks
2-inch piece of fresh ginger, peeled and cut into fine matchsticks
2 tablespoons light soy sauce
2 tablespoons vegetable stock
2 scallions, cut into 1-inch lengths
1 long fresh red chili, sliced diagonally into fine ovals
1/2 teaspoon granulated sugar
a pinch of salt
freshly ground black pepper, to taste

1 In a wok or frying pan, heat the oil and fry the garlic until golden brown.
Add the pork and mushrooms and stir well. Add the remaining ingredients in
turn, and stir-fry over a high heat until the pork is cooked through.

2 Season with black pepper and turn onto a serving dish.

for the noodles

1 nest of ba mee egg noodles (see page 24)

vegetable oil for deep-frying

for the vegetables

2 tablespoons vegetable oil

1 garlic clove, finely chopped

1 cup boneless chicken breast or thigh, cut into 1-inch strips

1/2 cup bamboo shoots (see page 19), finely sliced

1/3 cup straw mushrooms, whole, or cut in half if large

5-6 baby corns, cut in half lengthwise

1/2 small sweet red or green pepper, diced

2 scallions, cut into 1-inch lengths

1 tablespoon fish sauce

1 teaspoon dark soy sauce

1 teaspoon granulated sugar

1/2 teaspoon ground white pepper

1 tablespoon cornstarch, mixed with 1/2 cup vegetable stock or cold
  water to make a thin paste

for garnishing

a few fresh cilantro leaves

deep-fried noodles with chicken and mixed vegetables go see mee

This is very fast food, popular in bustling city business areas like the area off Silom Road near the Bangkok Bank headquarters. The noodles are deep-fried in advance, the sauce is steaming in its pot—the two ingredients simply have to be brought together, which takes a matter of seconds. It is an ideal party buffet dish, since it leaves the cook free to join in the fun while still proving that he or she has labored over a hot stove.

1 Separate the strands of egg noodle. Heat the oil to 400°F. in a deep-fat fryer and fry the noodles until crisp and golden brown. Remove and drain on paper towels, then place on a serving dish and keep warm.

2 In a wok or frying pan, heat the oil until a light haze appears. Add the garlic and fry until golden brown. Add all the remaining ingredients, stirring constantly, finishing with the thin cornstarch paste.

3 As soon as the mixture begins to thicken slightly, pour it over the crispy egg noodles. Garnish with fresh cilantro, and serve immediately.

fried wonton geeow tod

The whole point of fried wontons is that they're served crispy, so while they make good party food, they do have to be cooked at the last minute. When I was a child, there was a Chinese-Thai vendor who used to come down our soi with his wontons already fried. It was strange to us then that no matter how far or for how long he had been wandering around, his wontons were always crispy. Now that I've been in the restaurant business for years, I've learned that they will stay crisp if you keep them in an absolutely air-tight container. You can then serve them cold as long as you make sure the sauce is hot, to convince the diner that the wontons have just been cooked. I rather prefer them like that, which is no doubt because of my childhood memories.

for the sweet and hot sauces
6 tablespoons rice vinegar
1/4 cup granulated sugar
1/2 teaspoon salt
1 small red chili, finely chopped
1 small green chili, finely chopped

for the wonton wraps
1 garlic clove, roughly chopped
1 teaspoon roughly chopped cilantro root
1 teaspoon whole black peppercorns
1/2 teaspoon salt
1/2 teaspoon granulated sugar
3/4 cup ground pork
20 wonton wrappers (see page 21)
vegetable oil for deep-frying

1 To make the sweet and hot sauces, place the vinegar, sugar, and salt in a small saucepan, and stir over low heat until the sugar has dissolved. Let cool, then divide between 2 small serving bowls. Stir the chopped chilies into a bowl of sauce.

2 To make the wonton filling, pound the garlic, cilantro root, and peppercorns in a mortar to form a paste. Turn into a mixing bowl and stir in the salt and sugar. Add the ground pork and combine thoroughly with your hands.

3 Lay the wonton wrappers on a work surface and place a nugget of the filling in the center of each. Fold each square in half diagonally to make a triangle, brushing the edges with water to seal.

4 Heat the oil to 400°F. in a deep-fat fryer and fry the wontons until golden brown. Drain on paper towels and serve immediately, with the sweet and hot sauces.

southern salad salad kaek

for the salad

4 lettuce leaves

1 small onion, cut into rings

1/4 English cucumber, cut into very thin slices

1 cup bean sprouts

1 medium tomato, cut into wedges

for the sauce

2 tablespoons vegetable oil

1 garlic clove, finely chopped

1 tablespoon red curry paste (see page 25)

1/4 cup coconut cream

2 tablespoons crushed roasted peanuts

1 teaspoon granulated sugar

3 tablespoons light soy sauce

2 tablespoons lemon juice

3 tablespoons vegetable stock

for garnishing

1/2 4-ounce cake ready-fried tofu (see page 21), cut into 1-inch cubes

2 medium potatoes, sliced wafer thin, and deep-fried until crisp (or a package of potato chips)

1 Prepare the salad and set aside.

2 Heat the oil in a wok or frying pan and fry the garlic until golden brown. Add the curry paste and stir briefly. Pour in the coconut cream and bring to a boil, stirring well. Stir in the crushed peanuts, sugar, soy sauce, lemon juice, and vegetable stock. Remove from the heat and let cool completely.

3 To serve, either pour the sauce over the salad and garnish with tofu cubes and potato chips (do not toss the salad as this will be done by the diners), or serve each element separately.

shrimp wrapped in bean curd sheet heh guen

for the sweet and sour plum sauce

1/2 cup rice vinegar

1/2 cup granulated sugar

1 teaspoon preserved plum (see page 20), pitted

for the shrimp

2 garlic cloves, peeled

2 cilantro roots

1 cup peeled shrimp, coarsely chopped

2 tablespoons pork fat, finely chopped

ground white pepper, for seasoning

1 egg

4–5 bean curd sheets (see page 19), soaked in cold water for 8–10
  minutes until soft

vegetable oil for deep-frying

1 To make the sauce, combine the vinegar and sugar in a heavy pan and heat gently to dissolve the sugar. Bring to a boil and boil rapidly to make a thick syrup. Add the plum, breaking it up in the syrup with a metal fork. Pour into a small bowl and let cool.

2 To make the filling, pound the garlic with the cilantro roots in a mortar. Transfer to a mixing bowl and combine thoroughly with the chopped shrimp, pork fat, white pepper, and egg.

3 Lay the bean curd sheets on a work suface and divide the filling between each. Roll up to form "spring roll" shapes about five to six inches long, tucking in the ends. The bean curd sheets need to be handled carefully as they tend to tear, but you can patch them if necessary. You should finish with about three thicknesses of sheet around the shrimp filling.

4 Place the rolls in a steamer and steam for 10 minutes, during which time the bean curd will tighten around the filling. Remove from the steamer and let cool. The rolls can now be set aside for deep-frying later, or wrapped and stored in the refrigerator for frying the following day. They may also be frozen.

5 To finish, cut each roll into five to six rounds or into diagonal pieces. Heat the oil in a deep-fryer to 400°F. or until a light haze appears, and deep-fry the pieces until golden brown. Remove and drain on paper towels. Serve with the sweet and sour plum sauce.

hot fire morning glory
pak boong fi daeng

2 tablespoons vegetable oil

1 garlic clove, finely chopped

4 small fresh red or green chilies, finely chopped

1 tablespoon yellow bean sauce

1/2 pound morning glory, roughly cut into 2-inch lengths (about 2 cups)

1/4 cup vegetable stock

1 tablespoon light soy sauce

1 teaspoon granulated sugar

1 Heat the oil in a wok or frying pan. Add the garlic and chilies, and fry until the garlic is golden brown.

2 Add the yellow bean sauce, stir quickly, then add the morning glory, stirring once. Pour in the vegetable stock and simmer gently until the stems of the morning glory start to soften.

3 Season with the soy sauce and sugar, stir once, then turn onto a serving dish.

fried noodles with chicken
gueyteow koua gai

1 tablespoon vegetable oil

1 garlic clove, finely chopped

3/4 cup boneless chicken breast or thigh, finely sliced

1 egg

1 teaspoon chopped preserved radish (chi po, see page 20)

8 ounces (wet weight) soaked sen yai noodles (see page 24), drained and separated

1 tablespoon light soy sauce

a pinch of sugar

1 tablespoon fish sauce

1 large scallion, chopped

ground white pepper, for seasoning

lettuce leaves, for decorating

for garnishing

a sprig of fresh cilantro, coarsely chopped

1 Line a serving dish with roughly torn lettuce leaves and set aside.

2 Heat the oil in a wok or frying pan and fry the garlic until golden brown. Add the chicken and stir-fry over high heat until the meat is cooked through. Break the egg into the wok or pan and stir quickly. Add the remaining ingredients, one by one, stirring quickly after each addition. Make sure the noodles do not stick to the pan.

3 Turn the mixture onto a serving dish and garnish with fresh cilantro.

pork satay moo satay

(serves 4—see page 14)

So universal is satay in Thailand that it amazes people when I say that it used to be a rarity originally sold only by Muslim Malays traveling around the markets and festivals, mainly in the south. Although you did get a large bunch of them, traditional satay only had a tiny curl of meat—just enough for one dip of sauce before you put the whole thing in your mouth. Now they're everywhere and bigger, but not as much of a treat as they were.

for the pork skewers

1 pound lean pork steak, sliced into thin strips 4 inches x 1/2 inch

2 teaspoons coriander seeds

1/2 teaspoon cumin seeds

2 garlic cloves, roughly chopped

1-inch piece each of fresh ginger and turmeric, finely chopped

4 small red shallots, finely chopped

1 teaspoon salt

2 tablespoons granulated sugar

2 tablespoons vegetable oil

20 bamboo satay sticks

for the satay sauce

2 large dried red chilies, finely chopped

2 garlic cloves, finely chopped

1 stalk of lemongrass, finely chopped

1-inch piece of fresh turmeric, finely chopped

2 tablespoons vegetable oil

2 cups coconut milk

1 tablespoon tamarind water (see page 21)

2 tablespoons granulated sugar

1/2 teaspoon salt

1/4 cup crushed peanuts

1 In a mortar, pound together the coriander and cumin seeds, garlic, ginger, turmeric, and shallots to make a paste. Stir in the salt, sugar, and oil. Turn into a bowl, add the pork strips, and combine well to coat the meat thoroughly. Let marinate for 1 hour.

2 While the pork is marinating, make the satay sauce. In a mortar, pound together the chili, garlic, lemongrass, and turmeric to form a paste. Heat the oil in a wok or frying pan and stir in the paste. Add the coconut milk, stir well, and bring to a boil. Add the tamarind water, sugar, salt, and crushed peanuts, stirring between each addition. Simmer for three minutes, then pour into a serving bowl.

3 When the pork is marinated, fold each strip of meat in a ripple and pierce through the folds with a satay stick, as if sewing.

4 Place the sticks under a hot broiler or on a barbecue, turning from time to time, until cooked through. Serve with the sauce.

green chicken curry
gaeng kiow wan gai

Outside Thailand, this is the most popular of all the Thai curries. I'd be hard pressed to say why, but I must admit it's my favorite, too. Perhaps because it was one of my mother's specialties and my dad was always asking for it.

1/2 cup coconut cream

2 tablespoons vegetable oil

1 garlic clove, finely chopped

1 tablespoon green curry paste (see page 25)

2 tablespoons fish sauce

1 teaspoon granulated sugar

1 cup chicken breast or thigh, cut into thin strips

1/2 cup chicken stock

2 lime leaves, chopped

3 small green eggplants (see page 17), quartered

15 holy basil leaves

1 In a small pan, gently heat the coconut cream but do not boil. Set aside.

2 Heat the oil in a wok or frying pan, add the chopped garlic, and fry until golden brown. Add the curry paste and stir-fry for a few seconds. Add the warmed coconut cream and stir until it curdles and thickens in the oil. Stir in the fish sauce and sugar. Add the chicken strips and turn in the mixture until the meat becomes opaque.

3 Pour in the stock and simmer gently for three to four minutes, stirring occasionally.

4 Add the lime leaves, then stir in the eggplants and basil leaves. Cook for one minute more, then turn onto a serving dish.

steamed crabmeat
bu ja

Another street dish that is quick to prepare for busy city workers, the crab is already steamed in its shell and ready to eat.

3 garlic cloves, skinned

3 cilantro roots

a heaped 1/2 cup crabmeat

1/2 cup ground pork

1 egg

1 tablespoon fish sauce

1 tablespoon light soy sauce

1/2 teaspoon granulated sugar

3–4 crab shells or small ramekins, for serving

for garnishing

8 fine slivers red chili

8 fine slivers green chili

8 fresh cilantro leaves

1 Pound the garlic with the cilantro roots in a mortar to form a paste. Transfer to a mixing bowl and combine with the remaining ingredients, except the garnishes. Divide the mixture between the crab shells or ramekins, and place in a steamer. Steam for fifteen minutes.

2 Remove from the steamer and garnish with the slivers of red and green chili and the fresh cilantro leaves.

gold bags tung tong

for the dipping sauce
1/4 cup granulated sugar
1/4 cup rice vinegar
1/2 teaspoon salt
1 small red chili, cut into fine rings
1 small green chili, cut into fine rings

for the gold bags
1/2 cup ground pork
2 water chestnuts (see page 21), chopped
1 garlic clove, very finely chopped
ground white pepper, for seasoning
12 small wonton wrappers (see page 21), about 3 x 3 inches
vegetable oil for deep-frying

1 First make the dipping sauce. In a small saucepan, dissolve the sugar in the vinegar over low heat. Bring to a boil and boil rapidly, stirring, to give a pale golden syrup. Stir in the salt and the sliced chilies, and pour into a small bowl. (The sauce will thicken slightly as it cools.)

2 To make the filling, place the pork, water chestnuts, garlic, and a sprinkling of pepper in a mixing bowl, and combine well.

3 Lay the wonton wrappers on a work surface and place one teaspoon of the filling in the middle of each. Gather up the four corners with your fingertips and pinch them together to form a small bag.

4 To cook, heat the oil in a deep-fat fryer to 400°F. or until a light haze appears, and fry the wonton bags until crisp and dark golden brown. Drain on paper towels and serve with the dipping sauce.

rice soup khaotom

1 garlic clove, coarsely chopped
2 tablespoons vegetable oil
4 cups chicken stock
13/4 cups boiled fragrant rice
1/2 cup boneless chicken breast or thigh, thinly sliced
1/2 teaspoon chopped preserved vegetables (tang chi, see page 21)
1 tablespoon fish sauce
1 tablespoon soy sauce
1/2 teaspoon granulated sugar
1-inch piece of fresh ginger, finely chopped
1/2 teaspoon ground white pepper

for garnishing
1 scallion, finely sliced
a few fresh cilantro leaves

1 In a small pan, heat the oil and fry the garlic until golden brown. Remove from the heat and set aside the oil and garlic to infuse.

2 Heat the stock in a large pot, add the cooked rice and slices of chicken, and bring to a boil.

3 Stir in the remaining ingredients and simmer gently for about 30 seconds, or until the chicken is cooked through.

4 Pour into a serving bowl and drizzle a little of the reserved garlic oil on top. Garnish with finely sliced scallion and fresh cilantro leaves.

pork fried with red curry paste and long beans pad prik king moo

2 tablespoons vegetable oil

1 tablespoon red curry paste (see page 25)

1¼ cups pork tenderloin, finely sliced

1⅓ cups long beans (see page 17), cut into 2-inch lengths

2 tablespoons fish sauce

1 teaspoon granulated sugar

1 Heat the oil in a wok or frying pan, add the red curry paste, and stir well. Add the pork and stir-fry for a minute or two, until the meat is cooked through.

2 Add the beans, fish sauce, and sugar, stir thoroughly, then transfer to a serving dish.

steamed sticky rice with banana khao tom pad

This is handy traveling food because everything is wrapped in banana leaves, out of which the rice can be easily eaten—which is why you always find vendors with trays of them at long-distance bus terminals and train stations, or even walking down the corridors of the train cars themselves. Good for picnics when you don't want to haul plates and knives around.

1⅓ cups sticky rice (see page 22), soaked for 3–4 hours

2¼ cups coconut milk

½ teaspoon salt

¼ cup granulated sugar

5 small bananas, each about 4 inches long, cut in half lengthwise

banana leaves or tin foil, for serving (see page 15)

1 Drain the sticky rice and place it in a saucepan with the coconut milk. Bring up to simmering point, stirring constantly until the rice has just absorbed the liquid—about five to ten minutes. At this point, the rice will be half-cooked. Stir in the salt and sugar, then remove from the heat and let cool.

2 Make ten rectangles about 10 x 8 inches, out of banana leaf or tin foil. Place 2 tablespoons of half-cooked rice on each rectangle, flatten gently, then place a half-length of banana on top of each. Wrap up tightly by folding over first the long, then the short sides.

3 Place folded-side down in the upper compartment of a steamer and steam for half an hour. Serve in the leaf or foil wrapping, hot or cold.

Barbecued pork.

sticky rice with mango khao niew mamuang

This is easily the most popular Thai dessert, both with Thais who are great mango connoisseurs, and with Westerners, probably because it isn't as sweet as other Thai khanom, which can take a little getting used to. Sweet juicy mango served with rather firm sticky rice and slightly salty coconut cream is the perfectly balanced yin and yang combination. If you can get to Khun Pa Ni Chiapchalaart's street shop in Bangkok, you can sample this treat at its best.

1 cup plus 2 tablespoons coconut milk

2 tablespoons granulated sugar

1/2 teaspoon salt

2 1/4 cups sticky rice, cooked (see page 22) and still warm

4 ripe mangoes

2 tablespoons coconut cream

1 Combine the coconut milk and sugar in a small saucepan and heat gently, stirring all the time, until the sugar has dissolved. Do not let it boil.

2 Stir in the salt and warm, cooked, sticky rice, and set aside.

3 Peel the mangoes and cut off the two outer "cheeks" of each fruit, as close to the center pit as possible. Discard the pit. Slice each piece of fruit into four lengths.

4 Place a mound of sticky rice in the center of a serving dish, and arrange the slices of mango around it. Pour the coconut cream over the sticky rice and serve warm or cold.

When you leave the city, it can be difficult to find somewhere to eat. Don't worry, there is a solution. In Thailand, street food sellers can always be found near any public building. You can always have lunch or dinner when you visit a temple; they adorn many city streets and are found in every village. Fruit sellers nearby (like the one on the left), provide fruit for eating and to be used as gifts for the monks.

around bangkok

fish cakes with fresh pickle
tod man pla

(serves 4 – see page 14)

I tend to judge chefs by how well or badly they make this dish. The cakes have to be tender but not too soft—I know it sounds unappetizing, but the word "rubbery" springs to mind. The mixture should be kneaded gently but firmly, like a first class masseuse working on a tired muscle. Because street-sellers generally specialize in one dish and therefore get a lot of practice at it, I usually have this whenever I see it.

for the fresh pickle

1/2 cup rice vinegar

2 tablespoons granulated sugar

2-inch piece of English cucumber, unpeeled

1 small carrot

3 shallots, finely sliced

1 medium fresh red chili, finely sliced

1 tablespoon crushed roasted peanuts, for serving

for the fish cakes

5 dried red chilies, cut in half and seeded

1 shallot, finely sliced

2 garlic cloves, peeled

2 cilantro roots, roughly chopped

1 tablespoon finely chopped galangal (see page 17)

6 kaffir lime leaves, finely chopped

1/2 teaspoon salt

1 pound white fish fillet (cod, coley, haddock, or monkfish), minced for
  a few seconds in a food-processor

1 tablespoon fish sauce

1/2 cup long beans (see page 17) or green beans, sliced very fine

vegetable oil for deep-frying

1 To make the pickle, combine the vinegar and sugar in a small saucepan and heat gently until the sugar dissolves. Bring to a boil and boil rapidly for six to seven minutes, until a thin syrup is formed. Pour into a bowl and let cool.

2 Quarter the cucumber lengthwise, then slice finely across it. Cut the carrot in half lengthwise and slice finely across that. Add the cucumber, carrot, shallots, and chili to the cold syrup, and mix thoroughly. Set aside.

3 To make the fish cakes, pound the chilies, shallot, garlic, cilantro roots, galangal, kaffir lime leaves, and salt in a mortar to form a paste. Place the minced fish in a mixing bowl, add the paste, and combine thoroughly using your fingers. Mix in the fish sauce and finely sliced green beans, and knead firmly together. Divide into 20 balls and form into flat cakes about two inches across and a half inch thick.

4 Heat the oil in a deep-fat fryer to 400°F. and deep-fry the cakes until golden brown, about two to three minutes. Drain on paper towels, then arrange on a serving platter.

5 Sprinkle the crushed peanuts over the relish, and serve with the fish cakes.

chicken with holy basil
gai pad krapow

This dish can be prepared with chicken or beef.

2 tablespoons vegetable oil

2 garlic cloves, finely chopped

2 small fresh red or green chilies, finely chopped

3/4 cup ground chicken

1 medium onion, cut in half and roughly sliced

2 tablespoons fish sauce

1 tablespoon soy sauce

1 teaspoon granulated sugar

20 fresh holy basil leaves

1 In a wok or frying pan, heat the oil and fry the garlic and chilies, stirring well, until the garlic begins to brown.

2 Add the ground chicken and stir-fry over high heat, breaking apart the meat and mixing in the garlic and chili.

3 Add the remaining ingredients to the pan and continue to stir-fry until the chicken is cooked through. Turn onto a dish and serve.

rice noodles with coconut
meegrat ti

2 small shallots, peeled

8 black peppercorns

1 large red chili, roughly chopped

1/2 teaspoon salt

6 tablespoons coconut cream

3 tablespoons vegetable stock or water

1 teaspoon granulated sugar

1/2 teaspoon chili powder

2 tablespoons light soy sauce

4 ounces dry sen mee noodles (see page 24), soaked in water for
   about 20 minutes

1/2 4-ounce cake ready-fried tofu (see page 21), sliced into thin squares

2 cups bean sprouts

1 scallion, finely chopped

for garnishing
a few fresh cilantro leaves

1 Pound the shallots, peppercorns, chili, and salt in a mortar to form
a paste.

2 Warm the coconut cream in a saucepan or wok, but do not let it boil. Stir in the vegetable stock or water, the sugar, chili powder, and soy sauce. Add the paste from the mortar, stirring continuously until all the ingredients are blended together.

3 Strain the noodles and add to the sauce. Simmer gently until almost cooked through, then add the tofu, bean sprouts, and scallion. Mix quickly, turn onto a serving dish, and garnish with fresh cilantro leaves. Serve hot or cold.

chicken rice khao man gai

(serves 4 to 6—see page 14)

This dish is originally from Hunan Island in southern China. The Hunanese were very poor and emigration was common. The travelers took with them a simple, cheap cuisine of which this is the most famous example. It is now found all over southeast Asia, I suspect because anyone starting in the street food business doesn't need much capital outlay to start producing it. Anyway, like lots of simple peasant dishes, it is delicious, easy to find, and best of all for first time visitors to Asia, not too hot.

for the chicken

1 medium chicken, about 3 pounds
6 garlic cloves, lightly crushed
$1/2$ teaspoon salt
$2^2/3$ cups fragrant rice, rinsed

for the sauce

$1/2$ tablespoon yellow bean sauce
2-inch piece of fresh ginger, finely chopped
3 garlic cloves, finely chopped
5 small fresh red or green chilies, finely chopped
1 teaspoon dark soy sauce
2 tablespoons light soy sauce
2 tablespoons rice vinegar
1 tablespoon granulated sugar

for the accompaniment

$1/2$ English cucumber, sliced into rings
a large handful of fresh cilantro leaves, roughly chopped
2 scallions, finely chopped
ground black pepper, for seasoning

1 Place the chicken in a large pot and just cover with cold water. Remove the chicken from the pot and set aside. Add four of the garlic cloves, and the salt to the pan and bring to a boil. Place the chicken in the boiling water, cover with a lid, and boil for 20 minutes. Lower the heat, and simmer for a further 10 minutes. Remove the chicken and place on a rack to drain completely, reserving the water/stock.

2 Place the rice in a medium-sized pan and add enough of the chicken stock so that the liquid is an inch above the level of the rice. Add the 2 remaining garlic cloves, cover with a lid, and bring to a boil. Remove the lid, stir once, then replace the lid and let simmer very gently for 20 minutes without lifting the lid again. After this time, the rice should have absorbed all the liquid and be fluffy, with each grain separate. Remove from the heat, covered, and set aside.

3 Make the sauce. In a small bowl, mix together all the ingredients and set aside.

4 Prepare a small plate of sliced cucumber and chopped cilantro leaves, and set aside. Carefully carve the chicken into thin slices, retaining any skin but discarding the bones. Set aside.

5 Reheat the remaining stock and pour into individual soup bowls. Garnish with the finely chopped scallions and a little black pepper, and put on the table along with the bowl of hot sauce and the plate of cucumber and cilantro. Take a plate for each diner, place a good helping of rice on each, and arrange the slices of chicken on top. To serve, everyone eats their own rice and chicken and sips their own soup—or pours a little soup over their rice if they wish—while they share the sauce and cucumber.

barbecued pork with rice khao moo deang

(serves 6–see page 14)

Another dish of Chinese origin, simple, not-too-spicy, and easy to find—especially in pig-breeding areas like Nakhon Pathom, where this dish is a great specialty in the street food area around the giant temple (chedi).

for the barbecued pork

1/4 cup tomato paste

2 tablespoons dark soy sauce

1/4 cup light soy sauce

1/4 cup granulated sugar

21/4 pounds pork belly strips

22/3 cups fragrant rice, rinsed and drained

for the chili and vinegar sauce

1/4 cup rice or wine vinegar

1 small red chili, cut into thin rounds

for the salty sauce

2 cups pork stock

2 tablespoons light soy sauce

3 tablespoons granulated sugar

2 tablespoons fish sauce

1 teaspoon rice flour

for garnishing

1/4 English cucumber, thinly sliced

4 scallions, cut into 1-inch lengths

4 hard-boiled eggs, cut into quarters

1 Prepare the marinade by combining the tomato paste, soy sauces, and sugar in a large bowl. Add the pork belly strips and stir well to coat evenly in the sauce. Let marinate for one hour.

2 Cook the rice, drain and set aside.

3 Place the marinated pork belly strips on a barbecue or under a preheated broiler, turning them from time to time until cooked through.

4 While the pork is cooking, make the sauces. For the chili and vinegar sauce, combine the ingredients in a small bowl and set aside. For the salty sauce, heat the stock in a saucepan, add all the ingredients except the rice flour, and stir well. Bring to a boil and simmer for 1 minute. Sprinkle the rice flour over the liquid and whisk gently until the sauce thickens.

5 Cut the pork into very thin slices. (In the West, it is often cut too thickly, whereas in Asia, it is always cut as thinly as sliced ham.)

6 Put a heap of rice on each serving plate and top with thin slices of barbecued pork. Pour a good helping of the salty sauce on top. Garnish each plate with sliced cucumber, one or two short lengths of scallion, and a quartered hard-boiled egg. Serve with the chili and vinegar sauce.

fried river noodles with beef and dark soy pad si yew

1 tablespoon vegetable oil

2 garlic cloves, finely chopped

2/3 cup tender beef steak, finely sliced

1 egg

8 ounces (wet weight) soaked sen yai noodles (see page 24), drained

1 heaped cup broccoli, cut into small flowerets

1/2 teaspoon dark soy sauce

1 tablespoon light soy sauce

a pinch of sugar

2 tablespoons fish sauce

ground white pepper, for seasoning

chili powder, for seasoning (optional)

1 In a wok or frying pan, heat the oil and fry the garlic until golden brown. Add the beef and stir-fry over high heat to seal the juices. Break the egg into the pan and stir quickly until lightly set.

2 Add the noodles to the pan, tossing well to prevent them from sticking, then add the broccoli and stir again. Stir in the soy sauces, sugar, and fish sauce, then turn onto a serving dish. Season with a sprinkling of ground white pepper and chili powder, if using.

broiled fish with cilantro and garlic pla pow

6 cilantro roots

3 large garlic cloves, peeled

ground white pepper, for seasoning

1 mackerel or whiting, cleaned and patted dry inside and out

1 large banana leaf (see page 15) or tin foil

for garnishing

lettuce leaves

1 Pound the cilantro roots and garlic together in a mortar to form a paste, or blend in a food processor. Season the mixture with a generous shaking of ground white pepper.

2 Put this paste inside the cavity of the cleaned fish, then wrap the fish in a banana leaf or tin foil. If using a banana leaf, simply roll the wide leaf around the stuffed fish, fold the ends over, and secure with toothpicks. Preheat the broiler.

3 Broil the wrapped fish for about six to eight minutes on each side.

4 To serve, simply unwrap the fish and place on a bed of lettuce.

pork and fish ball noodles
gueyteow haeng moo

This is another quick dish—the street sellers usually ride on an adapted vehicle which is the back half of a bicycle, with a sort of wheeled box at the front. The box contains a pot of water, constantly on the boil, and a glass-fronted display case with noodles, and all the other ingredients and spices they need. All you have to do is flag the seller down and point. Anything you indicate will be put into a large strainer, which is dipped in the water for a few seconds, and then turned into a bowl. Effectively you are the chef, so you have no one to blame except yourself if it doesn't taste good.

2 tablespoons vegetable oil

2 garlic cloves, finely chopped

1 teaspoon chopped preserved vegetables (tang chi, see page 21)

1 tablespoon fish sauce

1 tablespoon light soy sauce

1/2 teaspoon granulated sugar

1/2 cup bean sprouts

8 ounces sen lek noodles (see page 24), soaked, drained, and separated

3 pork balls (see page 20)

3 fish balls (see page 19)

4 slices fish cake (see page 19)

4 slices cold boiled pork

1 tablespoon crushed roasted peanuts

1 sprig of fresh cilantro, coarsely chopped

1 In a wok or frying pan, heat the oil and fry the garlic until golden brown. Set aside to infuse, reserving the oil.

2 Put the preserved radish, fish sauce, soy sauce, and sugar into a deep serving bowl, mix quickly and set aside.

3 Bring a large pot of water to a boil. Using a wire-meshed ladle or a small coarse sieve with a handle, dip the bean sprouts into the boiling water for three seconds to just heat through. Turn the bean sprouts into the serving bowl, reserving the boiling water.

4 Dip the noodles into the boiling water in the same way—again, only for a few seconds—shaking them slightly to separate the strands. Drain, and add to the serving bowl. Pour one tablespoon of the reserved garlic and oil over them (this will help to separate the noodles, as well as adding flavor).

5 In turn, dip the pork balls, fish balls, and fish cake into the boiling water, heating them through completely before adding them to the serving bowl. Arrange the slices of cold pork (without heating them) over the noodles. To serve, sprinkle the dish with crushed peanuts and fresh cilantro, and mix quickly together. To turn this dish into noodle soup, simply pour in 2 cups of hot stock before garnishing with the peanuts and cilantro.

mussels in batter with egg hoy tohd

In Thailand, this is also made with oysters, which are just as cheap as mussels. This makes it popular with street sellers because it doesn't cost them much to start up in business. The consequence is that you find it everywhere—the public like it, too, mainly because it is very light and so, makes a good late night snack after a show or club.

for the chili-vinegar sauce
3 tablespoons rice vinegar
2 small chilies, finely sliced into rings
$^1/_2$ teaspoon granulated sugar

for the batter
3 tablespoons rice flour
3 tablespoons all-purpose flour
a pinch of salt
1 egg
a scant cup of water

for the mussels
6 ounces mussels, soaked, cleaned, de-bearded, and shelled
2 tablespoons vegetable oil, plus extra if necessary
1 egg
ground white pepper, for seasoning
1 tablespoon light soy sauce
1 tablespoon fish sauce
1 teaspoon granulated sugar
a handful of bean sprouts
1 scallion, coarsely chopped

for garnishing
a few fresh cilantro leaves

1 In a small bowl, mix all the ingredients for the chili-vinegar sauce together, and set aside.

2 To make the batter, combine the flours in a bowl and season with a pinch of salt. Make a well in the center, break in the egg, and add the water. Whisk thoroughly together, making sure there are no lumps—the mixture should have the consistency of thick cream.

3 Add the shelled mussels to the batter, coat thoroughly, and set aside.

4 In a large wok or frying pan, heat the oil, add the mussel and batter mixture, and tilt the pan from side to side to spread the mixture evenly over the surface. Cook the "pancake" for one to two minutes, then flip it over and cook the other side briefly until it is set. Divide the pancake into five or six portions using a spatula and a wooden spoon. Lower the heat and break the second egg into the pan. Quickly cook the pancake pieces in the egg, adding a little more oil if necessary. Stir in the bean sprouts and scallions, then season with a sprinkling of white pepper. Add the soy sauce, fish sauce, and sugar, turning the pancake pieces over quickly to absorb the liquid. Place on a warm serving dish and garnish with fresh cilantro. Serve with the sauce.

shrimp with lemongrass pla gung

lettuce leaves and parsley sprigs, for decoration

2 tablespoons lemon juice

2 tablespoons fish sauce

1/2 teaspoon chili powder

1 teaspoon granulated sugar

2 tablespoons stock

5–6 large shrimp, shelled and de-veined

1 lime leaf, finely chopped

1 shallot, coarsely chopped

1 stalk lemongrass, finely chopped

1/2 small onion, slivered

1 scallion, cut into 1-inch pieces

1 Line a small serving plate with lettuce leaves and sprigs of parsley, and set aside.

2 Put the lemon juice, fish sauce, chili powder, sugar, and stock in a small wok or frying pan, and boil rapidly for about a minute, stirring all the time until considerably reduced. Add the shelled shrimp and cook quickly until the shrimp are opaque. Add the remaining ingredients, stir once, remove from the heat, and transfer to the prepared serving plate. Serve immediately.

curried noodles gueyteow kak

1 4-ounce lean beef steak, cut into 1-inch cubes

1 hard-boiled egg

3 tablespoons vegetable oil

1 4-ounce cake ready-fried tofu, finely sliced

1 shallot, finely chopped

1 garlic clove, finely chopped

2 teaspoons red curry paste (see page 25)

¼ cup coconut milk

1 teaspoon curry powder

1 tablespoon fish sauce

1 teaspoon granulated sugar

2 ounces dry sen lek noodles (see page 24), soaked, drained,
  and separated

1 tablespoon crushed roasted peanuts

for garnishing
a few fresh cilantro leaves

1 Put the beef in a small pan and cover with water. Bring to a boil, then simmer gently for 10–15 minutes. Cut the egg into quarters and set aside. Heat a pan of water ready for the noodles.

2 In a small frying pan, heat one tablespoon of oil and fry the sliced tofu until slightly crisp. Drain and set aside, reserving the oil in the pan.

3 Reheat the oil (adding a little more, if necessary) and fry the shallot until dark golden brown and crisp. Set aside in the pan.

4 In a wok or large frying pan, heat two tablespoons of oil, add the garlic, and fry until golden brown. Stir in the curry paste and cook for a few seconds, then pour in the coconut milk and heat through. Do not let it boil.

5 With a slotted spoon or strainer, remove the beef from its pan (reserving the cooking liquid) and add to the curried sauce. Stir to make sure each piece is coated in the sauce. Add two cups of the cooking liquid (make up the amount with cold water if necessary), then add the curry powder, fish sauce, and sugar. Stir everything together and simmer gently for about five minutes.

6 Bring the water for the noodles to a boil. Put the noodles in a sieve or strainer with a handle, and dip them into the boiling water for two to three seconds, or until heated through. Drain, and divide between two serving bowls. Arrange the quartered egg on top of each bowl of noodles. Stir the crushed peanuts into the beef curry soup and pour on top of the noodles. Garnish with the reserved fried tofu, fried shallots with a little of their cooking oil, and the fresh cilantro.

Man cooking a late-night supper at the night market.

fried shrimp with chili and lime leaf
chu chee gung

2 tablespoons vegetable oil

2 garlic cloves, finely chopped

1 tablespoon red curry paste (see page 25)

2 tablespoons stock

6–8 raw king or tiger shrimp, shelled and de-veined

2 tablespoons fish sauce

1 tablespoon granulated sugar

1 tablespoon lemon juice

2 lime leaves, finely chopped

1 long red chili, finely slivered

1 Heat the oil in a wok or frying pan, add the garlic, and fry until golden brown. Stir in the curry paste and cook together for a few seconds. Add the stock and mix thoroughly. Toss in the shrimp and stir-fry for a few seconds until opaque.

2 Add the fish sauce, sugar, lemon juice, lime leaves, and chili, stirring after each addition. Cook together for 2–3 seconds, then turn onto a serving dish. This dish should be quite dry.

curried chicken steamed in banana leaf haw muk

If possible, you should use banana leaves to make the little cups in which the curried chicken is steamed. If you can't find any, use small heatproof bowls or ramekins, the size of a teacup, instead.

4 banana leaves or large ramekins

2 heaped tablespoons chopped Chinese cabbage

1 cup boneless chicken breast or thigh, cut into thin slices

2 teaspoons red curry paste (see page 25)

10 holy basil leaves

3 lime leaves, finely chopped

1 egg

2 tablespoons thick coconut milk

1 tablespoon fish sauce

for garnishing

2 tablespoons thick coconut milk

1 long red chili, finely chopped

1 First make the banana leaf cups. Cut the banana leaves into five-inch squares—you will need two squares for each cup. Place two squares, one on top of each other, on a work surface. Place a 4-inch bowl upside-down on top, and cut around the bowl to give two circles of banana leaf. Place the circles together, dull sides facing. Make a half-inch tuck about one and a half inches deep at any point on the circumference, and staple together. Repeat this at the opposite point. You will now have a slightly opened, squared-off cup.

2 Place a little Chinese cabbage in the bottom of each banana leaf cup, and set aside.

3 Place the chicken strips, red curry paste, basil leaves, chopped lime leaf, egg, coconut milk, and fish sauce in a bowl, and combine thoroughly.

4 Divide the mixture between the banana leaf cups, placing it on top of the chopped cabbage. Drizzle with a little coconut milk and garnish with red chili.

5 Place the cups in a hot steamer and cook for 20 minutes. Remove and serve.

fried taro pooak tod

Obviously popular with vegetarians, this could also be made with sweet potato.

for the taro

1 egg

1¹/₄ cups coconut milk

3 tablespoons all-purpose flour

¹/₂ teaspoon salt

1 tablespoon granulated sugar

1 tablespoon sesame seeds

10 ounces taro (see page 18), peeled and chopped into small chips
  about 1¹/₂-2 cups

vegetable oil for deep-frying

for the sauce

¹/₃ cup rice or white wine vinegar

¹/₄ cup granulated sugar

¹/₂ teaspoon salt

¹/₂ teaspoon chili powder

2 tablespoons crushed roasted peanuts

1 Combine the egg, coconut milk, flour, salt, sugar, and sesame seeds in a mixing bowl and whisk together to form a smooth batter. Add the taro chips, turning them well in the mixture until evenly coated.

2 To make the sauce, combine the sugar and vinegar in a small saucepan and heat gently until the sugar has dissolved. Bring to a boil and boil rapidly until the mixture thickens. Stir in the salt and chili powder, then remove from the heat and stir in the crushed peanuts. Pour into a serving bowl.

3 Heat the oil in a deep-fat fryer to 400°F. and deep-fry the battered chips until golden brown. Drain on paper towels and place on a serving dish. Serve with the sauce.

curried rice and chicken with fresh pickle (adjahd) khao mok gai

(serves 4 – see page 14)

This seems to have come north with Muslims from the South, which means it is probably Malay in origin.

for the chicken

1 medium chicken, weighing about 3–3¹/₂ pounds

3 tablespoons vegetable oil

4 large garlic cloves, finely chopped

2²/₃ cups fragrant rice, rinsed and drained

2 teaspoons each of curry powder and salt

2¹/₄ cups chicken stock

for the fresh pickle

¹/₄ cup rice vinegar

2 teaspoons granulated sugar

¹/₂ teaspoon salt

3-inch piece of English cucumber

2 small shallots, finely chopped

2–3 small fresh red chilies, thinly sliced

1 Cut the chicken in half, then chop each half into 3 equal pieces.

2 In a wok or frying pan, heat the oil and fry the garlic until golden brown. Stir in the rice, then add the curry powder and salt. Add the chicken pieces and stir well.

3 Either transfer the mixture to an electric rice-steamer, add the stock, cover, and cook for 20 minutes, or put the mixture in a heatproof bowl, add the stock, and place in the top part of a steamer over boiling water and steam for 30 minutes.

4 While the chicken is steaming, make the pickle. Warm the vinegar, sugar, and salt in a small pan, stirring until the sugar has dissolved. Remove from the heat. Cut the cucumber in half lengthwise, then cut it in half again and slice very finely. Add to the sauce along with the chopped shallots and chilies. Pour into a serving bowl and serve with the steamed chicken.

gold threads
foy tong

(serves 4–6 – see page 14)

This dish is often served at birthday parties or prepared as an offering to monks on special anniversary days. The look of the dish satisfies two of our desires—it is gold, a propitious color, and it has long threads indicating a long life. As a consequence, you'll find Foy Tong makers at most street food markets, especially if the market is near a monastery. To make the threads, you will need a special piece of equipment, made by cleaning a tin can and piercing the bottom with six small holes through which liquid can be streamed.

10 jasmine flowers
2 cups water
10 eggs
1 tablespoon vegetable oil
4 cups granulated sugar

1 Sprinkle the jasmine flowers over the water and let them infuse for one hour (see page 19).

2 Separate the egg yolks and reserve the whites. Whisk the yolks until thick and creamy, add the egg whites and the oil, and whisk again.

3 Remove the jasmine flowers from the perfumed water and discard. Pour the water into a large saucepan and add the sugar. Heat gently to dissolve the sugar, then boil rapidly to form a thin syrup.

4 To make the threads, fill your homemade strainer with the egg mixture and drizzle it in thin streams into the simmering sugar syrup, moving it in a circular motion to form nests of threads. Cook for one minute or until golden brown, then remove with a stick or skewer, and place on a metal tray to cool.

bananas in thick syrup
kruay chu'am

(serves 4–6 – see page 14)

1 cup granulated sugar
1 cup water
4 large bananas
1/2 cup coconut milk
1/4 teaspoon salt

1 Put the sugar and water in a heavy saucepan and heat gently until all the sugar has dissolved.

2 Peel the bananas and cut into two-inch pieces. Drop into the saucepan of boiling syrup, then lower the heat and cook gently until the bananas are bright and clear, and the sugar syrup forms threads when lifted with a wooden spoon. Remove any scum as it forms.

3 Serve with coconut milk, seasoned with salt to balance the sweetness.

coconut custard sankaya

1 cup granulated sugar

1 cup plus 2 tablespoons thick coconut milk

1 teaspoon rosewater

$^1/_2$ teaspoon salt

3 eggs, lightly beaten (use whites only, if you have some to use up)

1 Put the sugar and coconut milk in a large pan and heat gently until the sugar has dissolved. Stir in the rosewater and salt. Add the beaten eggs (or egg whites) and fold in carefully.

2 Pour the resulting custard into a heatproof bowl or metal baking tray. Place in the top of a preheated steamer and cook for 30 minutes, or until set. Cut into small squares, one to one and a half inches.

jackfruit seeds met kanoon

(serves 4–6 – see page 14)

These are little balls of sweetened bean paste and egg that are molded to look like jackfruit. Noon means something like "help and support," so this dish is aptly served at weddings.

1$^1/_3$ cups split mung beans (see page 19)

2$^3/_4$ cups dried coconut

1 cup granulated sugar

1$^1/_2$ cups water

2 egg yolks, beaten

1 Rinse the mung beans, place in a small saucepan, and cover with one and a half inches water. Cook gently for 30–45 minutes, or until completely soft.

2 Drain off any excess water and mash the beans thoroughly. Add the dried coconut and mix together to form a firm paste. Turn onto a work surface and divide into 20 pieces, each about the size of a small walnut. Shape into small "eggs."

3 Place the sugar and water in a large saucepan and heat gently until the sugar has dissolved. Bring to a boil and boil rapidly to form a thin syrup, the consistency of runny honey. Dip the "eggs" in beaten egg yolk and drop into the syrup for a few seconds, or until set. Remove with a small strainer and set on a wire rack to cool. Serve as candies.

baked mung bean and coconut custard kanom maw geang

(serves 6 – see page 14)

Phetchaburi is the "sweet tooth" town. Its surrounding sugar palms make it the center of the Thai confectionery trade, and lots of people make the short car journey to and from Bangkok at weekends and holidays to stock up with puddings and sweets. It has its own street food rags-to-riches story, with a woman called Mer Kim Li, who started making puddings like this dish, which she sold by the main road leading into the town. Soon her little trays of custard were famous and became the cause of special trips to Phetchaburi by eager Bangkokians. She went on to run a roadside shop, then a restaurant, and eventually a chain of them—all from something made out of a handful of beans!

2¹/₃ cups split mung beans (see page 19)

2 cups coconut cream

3 eggs, lightly beaten

2 cups granulated sugar

¹/₂ teaspoon salt

2 tablespoons vegetable oil

4 shallots, finely sliced

Night stall selling sweet noodles, Ayutthaya.

1 Rinse the mung beans in cold water. Place in a saucepan and cover with about two inches of water. Cook gently for 30–45 minutes, until the beans are completely soft.

2 Drain off any excess water and mash the beans to a smooth paste. Stir in the coconut cream, eggs, sugar, and salt. Pour the mixture into a shallow, greased baking pan, nine by nine by two inches, and bake in a medium oven (about 350°F.) for about an hour, or until golden brown on top and quite firm when pressed lightly.

3 While the pudding is baking, heat the oil and fry the sliced shallots until dark golden brown. Drain on paper towels and set aside.

4 Just before you take the pudding out of the oven, preheat the broiler. When the pudding is baked, set it under the broiler for about five minutes to crisp up the top. Let cool in the pan.

5 To serve, sprinkle with the fried shallots, then cut into small squares, one to one and a half inches.

A trip to the seaside for a group of Thai friends is always an excuse for a feast. Every popular beach area has a parade of itinerant food sellers, hawking fish and seafood specialties such as grilled squid, prawns in batter, and steamed mussels. Many walk up and down the beach with their *hahps*, while others congregate together to form beachside restaurants. Many visitors come for the food and not the ocean at all!

by the sea

three-flavored fish
pla sam rut

4 large garlic cloves, finely chopped

2 large fresh red chilies, finely chopped

1 medium-sized, firm-fleshed fish, suitable for deep-frying (bream or sea bass would do), cleaned

vegetable oil for deep-frying, plus 2 tablespoons extra for stir-frying

2 tablespoons palm sugar (see page 20)

3 tablespoons fish sauce

2 tablespoons tamarind water (see page 21)

1 In a mortar, pound the garlic and chilies together to form a paste. Set aside.

2 Rinse the fish and pat dry with paper towels.

3 Heat the oil for deep-frying to 400°F., and deep-fry the fish until golden brown and crispy. Drain on paper towels and place on a serving dish to keep hot.

4 Heat two tablespoons of oil in a wok or frying pan and stir in the pounded garlic and chili paste. Add the palm sugar and stir, then stir in the fish sauce and tamarind water. Pour on top of the deep-fried fish, and serve immediately.

hot and sour soup with shrimp and lemongrass tom yam gung

The pungent flavor of lemongrass has made this the most popular Thai soup. Actually, we don't eat it as soup, but instead pour a little on our rice as a flavoring while eating our main meal. I've put it in this chapter because we like to eat it when we arrive at the coast, since it clears the sinuses—the better to enjoy the bracing sea air.

2¼ cups chicken stock

1 tablespoon tom yam sauce (see page 26)

2 kaffir lime leaves, finely chopped

2-inch piece of tender lemongrass, roughly chopped

3 tablespoons lemon juice

3 tablespoons fish sauce

1–2 small fresh red or green chilies, roughly chopped

½ teaspoon granulated sugar

8 straw mushrooms, cut in half (canned mushrooms will do)

2 cups raw shrimp, peeled and de-veined

1 In a large saucepan, heat the stock with the tom yam sauce.

2 Add the lime leaves, lemongrass, lemon juice, fish sauce, chilies, and sugar, then bring to a boil and simmer for two minutes. Stir in the mushrooms and shrimp and cook for a further two to three minutes, or until the shrimp are cooked through.

3 Pour into soup bowls and serve.

steamed mussels with lemongrass
hoy op

If you like French moules marinières, you'll probably find this dish shares some of its qualities—not least that it has a light, refreshing flavor and is just as easy to cook. Another thing it shares with its French counterpart is that it is rather good served with a cold beer.

for the dipping sauce

2 tablespoons lemon juice

2 tablespoons fish sauce

1 teaspoon granulated sugar

4 small fresh red or green chilies, finely chopped

1 tablespoon crushed roasted peanuts

for the mussels

1 pound fresh mussels, soaked overnight in cold water, with a handful
  of oatmeal to aid the self-cleaning process

2 ounces lemongrass, cut into fine matchsticks (about 3/4 cup)

20 fresh holy basil leaves

1 First make the sauce. Place all the ingredients in a small serving dish and mix thoroughly. Set aside.

2 Next prepare the mussels. Rinse in clean cold water at least three times, then scrub thoroughly under cold running water, scraping off any barnacles or "beards." At every stage, discard any mussels that do not close when shaken, or which float to the surface of the water.

The author buying street food in Nakhon Pathom
before moving on to Hua Hin.

3 Place the mussels in a heavy pot on a high heat. Throw in the lemongrass and basil leaves and stir, then cover the pot with a lid. Shake the pot carefully from side to side, to toss the mussels in the liquid that has collected, and to spread the ingredients. Continue to cook for five to eight minutes, or until the shells have opened, shaking the pan occasionally.

4 Ladle on to a serving dish, discarding any mussels that haven't opened. To eat, remove the mussels from their shells, and dip in the sauce.

fried rice with pineapple
khao pad supparot

This is sometimes served in a scooped-out pineapple, either cut in half lengthwise, or hollowed-out whole with the top replaced. Its delicate sweetness makes it a particularly good accompaniment to seafood.

2 tablespoons vegetable oil

1 garlic clove, finely chopped

2 ounces dried black fungus mushrooms (see page 17), soaked in cold water for 10 minutes and cut into small pieces

1/2 cup chopped onion

1/2 cup pineapple chunks

1²/₃ cups cooked fragrant rice

3 tablespoons light soy sauce

1/2 teaspoon granulated sugar

1/2 teaspoon ground white pepper

1/4 cup roasted cashews

for garnishing

1 scallion, finely chopped into rings

a few fresh cilantro leaves

1 In a wok or frying pan, heat the oil until a light haze appears. Add the garlic, and fry until golden brown. Stirring all the time, add the mushrooms, onion, pineapple, rice, light soy sauce, sugar, and pepper.

2 Add the cashews, stir once, and turn onto a serving dish. Garnish with a sprinkling of scallion rings and fresh cilantro leaves, and serve.

puffed bread roti

3 cups all-purpose flour

2 tablespoons superfine sugar

1 egg, lightly beaten

1 cup cold water

6 tablespoons vegetable oil (you may not need all of this)

1 To make the dough, combine the flour and sugar in a bowl. Make a well in the center, break in the egg, and pour in the water. Combine everything together with your fingers, and knead to a smooth dough.

2 Divide the dough into ten balls. Using a rolling pin, press out each ball to make a round pancake—this should be as thin as possible, while still holding together when lifted from the counter.

3 Heat a griddle or frying pan, add enough oil to grease the surface and, when this is sizzling hot, fry the pancakes until crisp and golden brown, turning once. The Roti will puff up as they cook, creating a mottled effect with dark brown patches. Serve on their own as a snack; as an Indian-style accompaniment to curry; or as a dessert, dipped in sugar or condensed milk.

chicken with curry powder
gai pad pong kari

2 tablespoons vegetable oil

2 garlic cloves, finely chopped

1 teaspoon curry powder

2/3 cup chicken breast, cut into small pieces

1 small onion, chopped

1 medium potato, cut into small dice

about 1/2 cup stock or water

2 tablespoons fish sauce

a pinch of sugar

1/4 cup coconut milk

1 In a wok or frying pan, heat the oil and fry the garlic until golden brown.

2 Add the curry powder, stir to mix thoroughly, and cook for 1 minute. Add the chicken and stir well to coat the meat in the curry mixture. Add the onion, potato, and a quarter-cup stock, and stir-fry over medium heat until the potato is just cooked. If the mixture becomes dry, add a little more stock.

3 Stir in the fish sauce, sugar, and coconut milk, and simmer gently until the sauce thickens.

4 Turn into a bowl and serve.

fried rice with shrimp and chilies
khao pad prik gung

2 tablespoons vegetable oil

2 garlic cloves, finely chopped

2 small red chilies, finely chopped

1 cup peeled shrimp

1 tablespoon fish sauce

1/4 teaspoon granulated sugar

1 tablespoon light soy sauce

31/2 cups cooked fragrant rice

1/2 small onion, slivered

1/2 red or green sweet pepper, slivered

1/2 teaspoon ground white pepper

1 scallion, green part only, slivered into 1-inch lengths

for garnishing

a few fresh cilantro leaves

1 In a wok or frying pan, heat the oil and fry the garlic until golden brown.

2 Stir in the chilies and shrimp, then add the fish sauce, sugar, and soy sauce. Cook for a few seconds, stirring all the time, until the shrimp are cooked through.

3 Add the cooked rice and stir well, then add the onion, sweet pepper, white pepper, and scallion. Stir quickly to mix, then turn onto a serving dish and garnish with the fresh cilantro leaves.

deep-fried crab claws gam poo tod

for the plum sauce

1 whole preserved plum (see page 20)

1 cup rice vinegar or white wine vinegar

5 tablespoons granulated sugar

for the crab claws

1/3 cup ground pork

1 cup shelled and de-veined raw shrimp, finely chopped

1 egg

1 garlic clove, finely chopped

1 tablespoon fish sauce

1 tablespoon oyster sauce

1 teaspoon cornstarch

1/2 teaspoon ground white pepper

6–8 crab claws (depending on size)

vegetable oil for deep-frying

1 First make the plum sauce. With a fork, shred the flesh of the plum from its pit—this should leave you with tiny scrapings. Put the vinegar and sugar in a heavy saucepan and heat gently to dissolve the sugar. Bring to a boil and boil rapidly to make a syrup. Stir in the plum scrapings, then pour into a serving dish and set aside.

2 To make the coating for the crab claws, thoroughly mix together the ground pork, chopped shrimp, egg, garlic, fish sauce, oyster sauce, corn-starch, and white pepper. Divide the mixture by the number of crab claws (six to eight), and mold a piece around the meaty section at the end of each claw, leaving the pincer shell exposed.

3 Preheat the oil in a deep-fat fryer to 400°F. and fry the crab claws until the coating is deep golden brown. Remove, drain on paper towels, and serve with the plum sauce.

massaman lamb curry
massaman gae

Although near the sea, we often eat as much meat as seafood in the South—probably because much of the population is Muslim and we're keen to try their Malaysian dishes with unusual spices. Best known is massaman or "Muslim" curry, though it is now found all over Thailand.

1 cup plus 2 tablespoons coconut cream

2 tablespoons vegetable oil

1 garlic clove, finely chopped

1 tablespoon Massaman curry paste (see page 26)

6 ounces lean lamb, cut into 1-inch cubes

1 tablespoon tamarind water (see page 21) or 2 tablespoons lemon juice

1 teaspoon granulated sugar

3 tablespoons fish sauce

1 cup plus 2 tablespoons stock or water

2 small potatoes, quartered

2 tablespoons whole roasted peanuts

2 small onions, quartered

1 In a small pan, gently warm the coconut cream until it just starts to separate. Remove from the heat and set aside.

2 In a wok or frying pan, heat the oil and fry the garlic until golden brown. Add the curry paste, mix well, and cook for a few seconds. Add half the warmed coconut cream and cook for two to three seconds, stirring all the time, until the mixture bubbles and starts to reduce.

3 Add the lamb and turn in the sauce, to ensure that each piece is thoroughly coated. Stirring after each addition, add the tamarind or lemon juice, sugar, fish sauce, stock or water, and the remainder of the warmed coconut cream. Simmer gently for 15 minutes, stirring from time to time.

4 Add the quartered potatoes and simmer for a further four minutes. Add the peanuts and cook for four minutes more. Stir in the onions and cook for two more minutes, then pour into a serving dish.

hot and sour seafood salad
yam talay

lettuce, parsley, and cucumber slices, or other firm greens or raw vegetables in season

2 tablespoons lemon juice

2 small red chilies, finely chopped

2 tablespoons stock

1 teaspoon granulated sugar

2 tablespoons fish sauce

4 fish balls (see page 19)

4 large raw shrimp, shelled and de-veined

2–4 crab claws

4 pieces squid, cut into slices

2 lime leaves, finely sliced

1 shallot, finely chopped

1/2 small onion, finely slivered

a sprig of fresh cilantro, coarsely chopped

1 Prepare a seasonal salad and place in a serving dish. Set aside.

2 In a wok or frying pan, mix together the lemon juice, chilies, stock, sugar, and fish sauce. Bring to a boil, stirring all the time.

3 Add the fish balls, shrimp, crab claws, and squid, and stir-fry for a minute or two, or until cooked through. Remove from the heat and stir in the lime leaves, shallots, onion, and fresh cilantro. Pour on top of the prepared salad, and serve immediately.

squid with dry curry patpet plamuk

6-8 ounces squid (bodies only), washed and cleaned

2 tablespoons vegetable oil

2 garlic cloves, finely chopped

2 teaspoons red curry paste (see page 25)

1 tablespoon fish sauce

1 tablespoon light soy sauce

1 teaspoon granulated sugar

2–3 small green eggplants (see page 15), quartered

1 small red chili, finely chopped

2 lime leaves, finely sliced

10 holy basil leaves

1 Score the squid quite finely on both sides, then cut into pieces about an inch square.

2 In a wok or frying pan, heat the oil and fry the garlic until golden brown. Stir in the curry paste and cook for a few seconds. Add the squid, coating it in the sauce. Add the fish sauce, sugar, and eggplants, and stir-fry over a high heat until the eggplants are cooked through. Now stir in the chili, lime leaves, and basil.

3 When the squid is cooked through and opaque, give the dish a final stir and pour into a serving dish.

corn cakes
thod man khao phod

This is a vegetarian dish, normally served on the island of Phuket during the annual vegetarian festival—the largest in Thailand. Far from being a gentle herbivores reunion, the festival has some sort of strange religious basis that is marked by scenes of ritual self-punishment with participants walking through fire and sticking sharpened rods into themselves, all in a trance-like state. Definitely not for me.

for the cakes
1 tablespoon red curry paste (see page 25)
3/4 cup corn kernels (canned or frozen)
1 tablespoon light soy sauce
1 teaspoon granulated sugar
5–6 French beans or green beans, finely sliced
2 kaffir lime leaves, finely sliced
2 tablespoons dried breadcrumbs
vegetable oil for deep-frying

for the hot and sour peanut sauce
1/4 cup rice vinegar
2 tablespoons granulated sugar
1-inch piece of English cucumber, quartered lengthwise and
  finely sliced
2 shallots, finely sliced
1 tablespoon crushed roasted peanuts
1–2 small red chilies, finely sliced

1 Combine the ingredients for the corn cakes in a bowl and set aside.

2 To make the sauce, put the vinegar and sugar in a small saucepan and stir over low heat until the sugar has dissolved. Bring to a boil and boil rapidly until the sauce begins to thicken slightly. Remove from the heat, pour into a small bowl, and let cool completely.

3 Divide the corn mixture into 6 portions and form into small patties with your hands.

4 Heat the oil in a deep-fat fryer to 400°F. While the oil is heating, stir all the remaining sauce ingredients into the syrup and set aside.

5 Fry the patties in the hot oil until golden brown. Remove, drain on paper towels, and serve with the sauce.

shrimp spring rolls po pea gung

To me, this is just one of many pleasant, simple, inexpensive nibbles you get on most beaches in Thailand—although I must admit its rather elegant appearance makes it look classier than the average snack. You can now find it on the menu at many fashionable restaurants—and at highly-inflated prices.

for the marinade
2 large garlic cloves, finely chopped
1 tablespoon fish sauce
1 tablespoon light soy sauce
1 tablespoon oyster sauce
1/2 teaspoon white pepper
1 teaspoon granulated sugar

for the spring rolls
10 large raw king shrimp, shelled and de-veined
10 spring roll sheets, about 3 inches square
vegetable oil for deep-frying

for the sweet chili sauce

¹/₄ cup granulated sugar

6 tablespoons rice or white wine vinegar

¹/₂ teaspoon salt

2 small red chilies, finely chopped

1 Combine the ingredients for the marinade in a bowl, stir in the shrimp, coating them well in the sauce, and let marinate while you complete the other tasks.

2 To make the chili sauce, put the sugar and vinegar in a small saucepan and heat gently until the sugar dissolves. Bring to a boil and boil rapidly until the sauce starts to thicken. Remove from the heat, stir in the salt and chopped chili, and pour into a small bowl. Set aside.

3 Lay the spring roll sheets on a counter. Place a marinated shrimp in the center of each sheet and roll up, as illustrated in the photograph.

4 Heat the oil to 400°F. in a deep-fat fryer. Fry the spring rolls until pale golden brown, then remove and drain on paper towels. Serve with the sweet chili sauce.

stir-fried seafood with garlic and peppercorns

talay pad kratiam prik thai

This is one of those dishes that turns the economics of cooking completely on its head, and is reason enough to visit Thailand. In the West, seafood is expensive and fresh peppercorns prohibitively so, yet somewhere like the street food market along the road leading up to the old Railway Hotel in the seaside resort of Hua Hin, it costs only a few coins. As they say in the Michelin guides: "worth the detour."

2 tablespoons vegetable oil

3 garlic cloves, finely chopped

3 ounces squid, cleaned and cut into 3/4-inch pieces (about 1/2 cup)

4 king shrimp, shelled and de-veined

4 scallops

4 crab claws

1 tablespoon fish sauce

1 tablespoon oyster sauce

1 tablespoon light soy sauce

1/2 teaspoon granulated sugar

1/2 teaspoon white pepper

1/3 cup fresh green peppercorns

1 In a wok or frying pan, heat the oil and fry the garlic until golden brown.

2 Add the seafood and the remaining ingredients, and stir-fry over high heat for two to three minutes. Transfer to a serving dish.

barbecued squid plamuk yang

Sold on nearly every beach around Thailand, the aroma of grilling squid instantly evokes sea, sand, and holidays. At the seaside, I always have some at the end of the day with a beer or a whisky, as an aperitif before my evening meal.

2 large squid (bodies about 6-9 inches long), cleaned, with the sac and tentacles separated

for the three-flavor sauce

2 tablespoons fish sauce

3 tablespoons lemon juice

2 large garlic cloves, finely chopped

2 small green chilies, finely chopped

2 teaspoons granulated sugar

1 Preheat the barbecue or broiler.

2 Cut each squid body sac lengthwise into quarters and rinse under a tap. With a sharp knife, lightly score each side of the squid body diagonally into a diamond pattern (this will help the cooking process and make the final dish more attractive). Leave the tentacles whole for broiling—although they can be cut up after cooking.

3 Lay all the squid pieces under the broiler and cook for about 10 minutes on each side, or until well-browned; the body pieces should curl up.

4 While the squid is cooking, make the sauce. Combine the fish sauce, lemon juice, chopped garlic, chilies, and sugar in a small bowl and set aside.

5 To serve, arrange the cooked squid on a large dish and place the bowl of sauce in the middle. Dip the squid pieces into the sauce and eat with your fingers.

shrimp in batter with two sauces
gung tod

You may not intend to eat on the beach, but when these turn up, carried on a tray by a strolling vendor, it's surprising how they whet the appetite. The batter and sauces are also suitable for making deep-fried tempura vegetables—carrots, celery, beans, and zucchini all work well.

for the chili-vinegar sauce
1/4 cup rice vinegar
1/4 cup granulated sugar
1/4 teaspoon salt
1 small red or green chili, finely chopped

for the cilantro-soy sauce
3 tablespoons light soy sauce
5–6 fresh cilantro leaves, coarsely chopped

for the shrimp in batter
1 1/4 cups all-purpose flour
1/2 teaspoon salt
1 egg
1 cup water
vegetable oil for deep-frying
12 large shrimps, heads removed, shelled, and de-veined (but with tail shell on)

1 First make the chili-vinegar sauce. Put the vinegar and sugar in a small saucepan and heat gently, stirring, until the sugar dissolves. Bring to a boil and boil rapidly to form a syrup. Stir in the salt, remove from the heat, and pour into a serving dish to cool. Add the chopped chili.

2 To make the chili-vinegar sauce, combine the soy sauce with the cilantro leaves and pour into a small bowl.

3 For the batter, combine the flour and salt in a bowl. Make a well in the center and break in the egg. Add the water gradually, whisking constantly, to give a thick, creamy batter.

4 Heat the oil in a deep-fat fryer to 400°F. or until a light haze appears. Dip each shrimp into the batter, making sure it is thoroughly coated, and drop into the hot oil. Deep-fry until golden brown. Remove with a strainer or slotted spoon, and drain on paper towels. Arrange on a serving dish.

5 To eat, hold the shrimp by the tail and dip into either sauce.

beancurd sheet stuffed with crab

hoi joh

For the crab wraps

4–5 beancurd sheets, about 6 x 12 inches (see page 19)

3/4 cup crabmeat

1/4 cup ground pork

2 garlic cloves, finely chopped

1 egg

1 tablespoon light soy sauce

1/2 teaspoon ground white pepper

1 teaspoon granulated sugar

a pinch of salt

vegetable oil for deep-frying

for the plum sauce

1 small preserved plum (see page 21)

6 tablespoons rice or white wine vinegar

1/4 cup granulated sugar

for garnishing

lettuce leaves and finely sliced cucumber

1 Soak the beancurd sheets in cold water for five to six minutes, or until soft and pliable. (Handle with care as they are prone to tearing.) Set aside.

2 To make the filling, combine the crabmeat, pork, garlic, egg, soy sauce, pepper, sugar, and salt in a bowl.

3 Place the soaked beancurd sheets on a counter and divide the filling between each. Roll the sheets up to form sausage shapes, folding in the ends. You should end up with four to five wrapped sausages about four inches in length. Tie the wraps at intervals with cotton thread to divide into four to five sections. Place in a preheated steamer and steam for 10 minutes, during which time the beancurd will tighten around the filling.

4 Remove from the steamer and let cool. If you are preparing the Hoi Joh in advance, you can now place the wraps in the refrigerator for cooking later that day, or even the following day. They may also be frozen at this stage.

5 To make the plum sauce, place all the ingredients in a small saucepan and heat gently, stirring, until the sugar has dissolved. Bring to a boil and boil rapidly to form a thin syrup. Check for flavor—the sauce should be sweet and sour—and pour into a serving dish.

6 To finish, cut the beancurd wraps where they are tied with cotton and remove the thread. You will now have 16–20 roughly ball-shaped pieces. Preheat the oil for deep-frying to 400°F. and fry the pieces until golden brown. Arrange the deep-fried balls on a serving plate lined with lettuce and finely sliced cucumber, and serve with the sauce.

clams with chili and basil

hoy lai pad nam prik pow

1 pound fresh baby clams in their shells

2 tablespoons vegetable oil

2 garlic cloves, finely chopped

1 tablespoon grilled chili oil (nam prik pao, see page 26)

2 tablespoons fish sauce

2 tablespoons stock or water

$1/2$ teaspoon granulated sugar

1 long red chili, finely slivered

20 holy basil leaves

1 Rinse the clams under cold water, discarding any that do not close when shaken. Drain and set aside.

2 In a wok or frying pan, heat the oil and fry the garlic until golden brown. Add the clams and grilled chili oil and stir thoroughly. Add the remaining ingredients in turn, stirring after each addition, and cook over high heat until the clams open. Discard any clams that remain closed.

3 Pour into a serving bowl and serve.

stir-fried seafood with roast chili paste talay pad prik pao

2 tablespoons vegetable oil

3 garlic cloves, finely chopped

1 tablespoon grilled chili oil (nam prik pao, see page 26)

4 king shrimp, shelled and de-veined

4 scallops

4 mussels

4 crab claws

1 ounce (about 1/4 cup) squid, cut into 3/4-inch pieces

1 stalk celery, sliced

1 carrot, about 1 1/2 inches long, cut into slices

3 tablespoons mixed red, yellow, and green sweet peppers, sliced

1 tablespoon oyster sauce

1 tablespoon fish sauce

1 teaspoon granulated sugar

1 In a wok or frying pan, heat the oil and fry the garlic until golden brown.

2 Add the chili oil and stir well, then toss in the seafood and stir-fry for about two minutes.

3 Add the vegetables and the remaining ingredients, and stir-fry for one minute more. Transfer to a serving dish and serve.

sweet and sour tofu tao hou peaw wan

This is a classic vegetarian dish served on its own, but its light, varied flavors also make it good to serve with seafood dishes, particularly hot ones like Stir-fried Seafood with Roast Chili Paste (see recipe opposite).

vegetable oil for deep-frying, plus 2 tablespoons for stir-frying

1 4-ounce cake of tofu (see page 21), cut into 2 inch cubes

2 garlic cloves, finely chopped

3 tablespoons English cucumber, sliced

3 tablespoons mixed red, yellow, and green sweet peppers, sliced

3–4 white mushrooms, quartered

4–5 whole baby corns, quartered lengthwise

2 scallions, cut into 3/4-inch lengths

3 tablespoons pineapple chunks

1 medium tomato, cut into round pieces

2 tablespoons granulated sugar

2 tablespoons white wine vinegar

1 teaspoon salt

1 Put the tofu on a board and place a weight (e.g., a pan of water) on top of the tofu. Angle the board so the compressed tofu will drain into the sink, leave it for an hour or longer, to try to squeeze as much liquid out as possible, so it won't splutter later when put in the deep-fat fryer.

2 Heat the oil to 400°F. in a deep-fat fryer. Deep-fry the tofu cubes until golden brown, remove, and drain on paper towels.

3 In a wok or frying pan, heat the oil and fry the garlic until golden brown. Add the vegetables, stir well, then add the sugar, vinegar, and salt. Stir-fry over high heat for 30 seconds.

4 Toss in the deep-fried tofu, stir once, then turn onto a serving dish.

the north

Bangkokians love to go to Chaing Mai because of the cool climate, but the food is the real draw. Here we see a parade of boys dressed in historical military costumes, resting by a stall selling sweets during the Inthakin Festival at Wat Chedi Luang.

chiang mai spicy dip
nam prik num

The Thai language is full of double meanings. In this dish, for example, "Num," can also mean a young man, so the recipe calls for young chilies, which are thought to be particularly lusty.

2 large fresh green chilies

4 small fresh green chilies

4 large garlic cloves, peeled

4 small shallots, peeled

2 medium tomatoes

5 round green eggplants (see page 17)

2 tablespoons lemon juice

2 tablespoons fish sauce

1/2 teaspoon salt

1 teaspoon granulated sugar

1 Preheat the broiler.

2 Wrap the chilies, garlic, shallots, tomatoes, and eggplants in foil, and place under the broiler. Cook until they begin to soften, turning once or twice. Unwrap, place in a mortar, and pound together to form a liquid paste.

3 Add the lemon juice, fish sauce, salt, and sugar to the paste, stirring well.

4 Turn into a small bowl. Serve as a dip, surrounded by crisp salad ingredients—crisp lettuce, cucumber, radish, and celery—or with raw or blanched vegetables.

curried pork with pickled garlic
gaeng haeng lay

This shows the influence of neighboring Burma and, through Burma, of India, on Thai cuisine. There are many Burmese cultural influences in the northwest, particularly on religious ceremonies but also on craftwork such as woodcarving, at which the Burmese excel. Indeed, many of the things on sale in northern Thai craft shops may have been made in Burma and smuggled across the border.

2 tablespoons vegetable oil

1 garlic clove, finely chopped

1 tablespoon red curry paste (see page 25)

1/2 cup coconut cream

4 ounces boneless pork with a little fat, finely slivered (about 1/2 cup)

1-inch piece of fresh ginger, peeled and finely chopped

2 tablespoons chicken stock or water

2 tablespoons fish sauce

1 teaspoon granulated sugar

1/2 teaspoon turmeric powder

2 teaspoons lemon juice

4 pickled garlic cloves (see page 20), finely chopped

1 In a wok or frying pan, heat the oil and fry the garlic until golden brown. Add the curry paste and stir well. Pour in the coconut cream and stir until the liquid begins to reduce and thicken. Do not boil.

2 Add the pork and stir-fry over high heat until cooked through—approximately one minute. Add the remaining ingredients in turn, stirring constantly.

3 Turn into a serving bowl and serve.

chicken curry noodle with pickled cabbage kow soi

Originally from Burma, this has become the single most popular dish in and around the northern Thai capital Chiang Mai. This is where each of my friends seems to have his or her favorite street seller, who they insist I visit. They get quite passionate in defense of their vendor and we often end up arguing by the road as to where we should eat—much the most enjoyable sort of argument to have.

4 ounces fresh ba mee noodles (see page 24), or use 2 ounces dry noodles, soaked and drained

2 tablespoons vegetable oil

1 small garlic clove, finely chopped

1 teaspoon red curry paste (see page 25)

1/2 cup coconut cream

6 ounces boneless chicken breast or thigh, cut into thin strips (about 1 heaped cup)

1 cup chicken stock

1 teaspoon curry powder

2 tablespoons fish sauce

1/2 teaspoon lemon juice

1/2 teaspoon granulated sugar

for garnishing

1 scallion, coarsely chopped

2 shallots, finely diced

1 tablespoon pickled cabbage (pat gat dong, see page 20), thinly sliced

1 lemon, cut into wedges

1 Bring a pot of water to a boil. Using a sieve or mesh strainer, dip the noodles into the water for two to three seconds, just to heat them through. Drain, and set aside in a serving bowl.

2 In a wok or frying pan, heat the oil and fry the garlic until golden brown. Stir in the curry paste and cook for a few seconds. Pour in the coconut cream and cook until the liquid starts to reduce and thicken. Do not boil. Add the chicken and stir-fry for a minute or two, then add the chicken stock, curry powder, fish sauce, lemon juice, and sugar, stirring constantly.

3 Pour the chicken mixture over the noodles, garnish with scallion, shallots, and pickled cabbage and serve with the lemon wedges on the side. Good with sticky rice when you're traveling, as it can be eaten cold with fingers, so look out for it at transport stops.

A line of food stalls, lit up for the night, in front of Wat Pan Tow.

deep-fried spare ribs grat dook moo tod

4 garlic cloves, roughly chopped

4 large cilantro roots, roughly chopped

2 tablespoons all-purpose flour

1 egg

2 tablespoons fish sauce

2 tablespoons light soy sauce

1 pound pork spare ribs, chopped into 1½–2-inch pieces

vegetable oil for deep-frying

1 Using a mortar and pestle, or a blender, pound or blend the garlic and cilantro roots together, and set aside.

2 In a large bowl, mix together the flour with the egg, fish sauce, and soy sauce. Add the garlic and cilantro paste and mix thoroughly. Add the spare rib pieces and coat well with the mixture. Let marinate for at least half an hour.

3 Heat the oil to 400°F. in a deep-fat fryer or until a light haze appears. Fry the pieces of spare rib for six to eight minutes, or until dark golden brown. Remove with a slotted spoon, drain on paper towels, and serve.

fried fish with turmeric
pla tod khamin

This is usually made with freshwater fish. In the north, vendors lay the fish out in a line for you to choose from, and give you the sauce in a little plastic bag so that you can pour it over the fish when you want. Surprisingly, though it's cold, the fish is still crispy. It's another useful dish for travelers with limited equipment, though you will need a spoon.

1 medium-sized, firm-fleshed fish (bream or sea bass would do) or
  2 fillets
2-inch piece of fresh turmeric (see page 18), roughly chopped
1 tablespoon peppercorns
2 large garlic cloves, roughly chopped
1 tablespoon roughly chopped shallots
1 tablespoon fish sauce
1 tablespoon granulated sugar
3 tablespoons vegetable oil

for garnishing
a few fresh cilantro leaves

1 Clean the fish and cut into two-inch pieces.

2 In a mortar, pound together the turmeric, peppercorns, garlic, and shallot to form a paste.

3 Place the pieces of fish in a bowl with the paste, fish sauce, and sugar. Mix well, spreading the paste all over the fish.

4 Heat the oil in a frying pan and fry the fish until crisp and golden brown.

5 Drain on paper towels and arrange on a serving dish. Garnish with fresh cilantro and serve.

fried rice with pork
khao pad moo

1 tablespoon vegetable oil
2 garlic cloves, finely chopped
4 ounces lean pork, finely slivered (about 1/2 cup)
1 egg
1 3/4 cups cooked fragrant rice
1 heaped cup broccoli, cut into small flowerets
1 tablespoon light soy sauce
a pinch of sugar
1 tablespoon fish sauce
ground white pepper, to season

1 Heat the oil in a wok or frying pan, add the garlic, and fry until golden brown.

2 Add the pork and stir-fry briefly over high heat. Break the egg into the pan and stir well. Add the rice, combine well, then stir in the broccoli.

3 Stirring constantly, add the soy sauce, sugar, and fish sauce. Turn onto a serving dish, season with ground white pepper, and serve.

fried curried rice

khao pad pong karl

2 tablespoons vegetable oil

1 garlic clove, finely chopped

1³/₄ cups boiled rice

¹/₂ cup potato, cut into ¹/₂-inch dice

¹/₂ cup onion, cut into small dice

¹/₂ cup peas

3 tablespoons light soy sauce

¹/₂ teaspoon granulated sugar

1 teaspoon curry powder

¹/₂ teaspoon ground white pepper

for garnishing

1-inch piece of English cucumber, finely sliced into round pieces

a few fresh cilantro leaves

1 In a wok or frying pan, heat the oil until a light haze appears, add the garlic, and fry until golden brown. Add the boiled rice, stir once, then add all the remaining ingredients and stir-fry until the potato is cooked through.

2 Turn onto a serving dish and garnish with sliced cucumber and fresh cilantro.

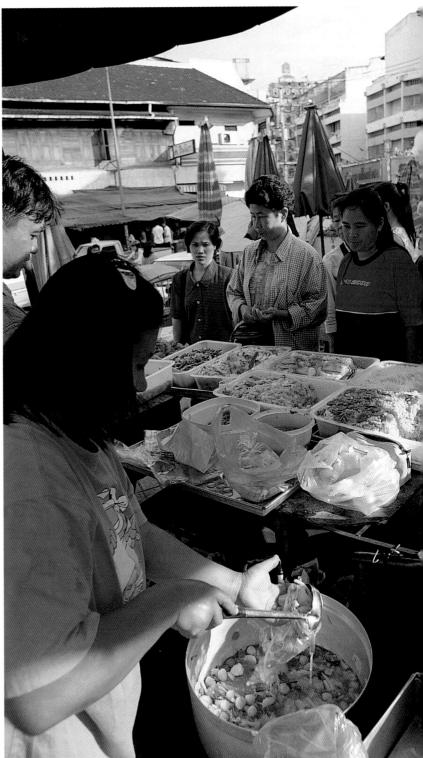

Woman preparing fish ball soup at the Long Yan Market (*Talat Lam Yai*), Chiang Mai.

egg noodles with stir-fried vegetables mee sua

2 tablespoons vegetable oil

1 garlic clove, finely chopped

1 large red dry chili, roughly chopped

4 ounces ba mee noodles (see page 24), dried or fresh

1/2 cup celery, finely chopped

1 cup bean sprouts

2 scallions, finely chopped

1 medium tomato, cut into segments

1/2 teaspoon chili powder

3 tablespoons light soy sauce

1 teaspoon dark soy sauce

1/2 teaspoon granulated sugar

1 Bring a pot of water for the noodles to a boil. If using fresh noodles, shake the strands loose, place in a sieve or strainer, and lower into the boiling water for two to three seconds, or until heated through. If using dried noodles, cook in the boiling water until the strands separate, by which time they will be soft. Drain and set aside.

2 In a wok, heat the oil until a light haze appears. Add the garlic and fry for a moment, then add the chili and continue to stir-fry until the garlic is golden brown.

3 Add the cooked noodles to the pan, stir well to prevent them from sticking, then add the remaining ingredients, stirring quickly. Turn onto a serving dish and serve.

white radish cake with bean sprouts kanom pad ga

(serves 3–4, see page 14)

This recipe is prepared in two distinct stages: first the cake is made, then it is re-cooked with bean sprouts, as here, or with other ingredients. This dish goes well with Prik Nam Som (see page 24) or Sriracha Chili Sauce.

for the cake

1 white radish (mooli, see page 18), weighing about 2 pounds

1¹/₂ cups rice flour

2 tablespoons all-purpose (wheat) flour

2 tablespoons water

1 Trim and peel the radish and cut into small cubes. Using a food processor or blender, grind the radish as finely as possible. This will have to be done in two to three batches. Place the ground radish in a bowl and mix thoroughly with the rice and wheat flours, and water.

2 Turn the mixture into a shallow pan or heatproof dish, about 8 inches square: it should come about an inch up the sides. Heat up your steamer (or use your largest pot with an upturned bowl in the bottom, on which to rest the pan) and steam the cake for about 30 minutes from the time the steamer is hot. If you are using a thicker dish, you will have to steam the cake for a little longer. When an inserted knife comes out clean, remove from the heat and let cool and dry out completely. The cake will set more solidly as it cools.

3 To serve, cut the cake into rectangles about one by two inches square.

to finish the dish

3 tablespoons vegetable oil

¹/₂ batch white radish cakes, cut into rectangles (see opposite)

2 garlic cloves, finely chopped

1 egg

2 tablespoons light soy sauce

1 tablespoon dark soy sauce

¹/₂ teaspoon granulated sugar

ground white pepper, to season

¹/₂ cup fresh bean sprouts, rinsed and drained

3 scallions, cut into 1-inch slivers

1 In a frying pan (preferably non-stick), heat half the oil. Add the radish cake pieces and, stirring and turning constantly, fry until they are browned on all sides. Remove from the pan and set aside.

2 Add the rest of the oil to the pan and fry the garlic until golden brown. Break in the egg and cook for a few seconds, stirring all the time until the egg starts to set. Add the fried radish cake and mix well. Stir in both soy sauces, the sugar, pepper, bean sprouts, and scallions, then turn onto a serving dish.

note

The remaining radish cake can be fried with other ingredients.

pork fried with chili and nuts
moo pad prik haeng

2 tablespoons vegetable oil

1 garlic clove, finely chopped

5–6 dried long chilies, with or without seeds, chopped

4 ounces lean pork, finely sliced (about 1/2 cup)

1 tablespoon fish sauce

1 heaped tablespoon whole roasted peanuts

6–8 small thin French beans or green beans, cut into 1-inch lengths

3 tablespoons stock

1 tablespoon light soy sauce

1/4 teaspoon granulated sugar

1 In a wok or frying pan, heat the oil and fry the garlic until golden brown. Add the chilies and stir. Add the pork and stir-fry over high heat until the meat is slightly opaque.

2 Add the remaining ingredients, one by one, stirring after each addition. Cook for another minute or two, making sure the meat is cooked through, and turn onto a serving dish.

Men selling trays of fried insects, with the tower of Wat Mahawan in the background.

ground beef noodle with curry
powder gueyteow nua sap

3 tablespoons vegetable oil

8 ounces (wet weight) soaked sen lek noodles (see page 24), rinsed and separated

1 teaspoon dark soy sauce

1 garlic clove, finely chopped

1/2 cup lean ground beef

1 tablespoon chopped preserved radish (chi po, see page 24)

3 tablespoons stock, plus extra if necessary

1/2 teaspoon curry powder

1 small onion, finely slivered

1 tablespoon fish sauce

1 teaspoon cornstarch, mixed to a thin paste with water (you may not need all of this)

1 small scallion, finely chopped

1 sprig of fresh cilantro, coarsely chopped

for serving

lettuce, for decoration

1 Line a serving dish with roughly-torn lettuce.

2 Heat 2 tablespoons oil in a wok or frying pan. Add the noodles, stir quickly to prevent them from sticking, then add the dark soy sauce. Stir-fry for 30–60 seconds, then turn onto the prepared serving dish and set aside.

3 Add one more tablespoon of oil to the pan, add the garlic, and fry until golden brown. Add the beef and stir-fry over high heat until the beef loses its

shrimp with ginger
gung pad king

Even in the extreme North, seafood is very popular.

2 tablespoons vegetable oil

2 garlic cloves, finely chopped

1-inch piece of fresh ginger, finely sliced

6–8 large shrimp, peeled and de-veined

1/4 teaspoon ground white pepper

1 tablespoon light soy sauce

1 tablespoon fish sauce

1/2 teaspoon granulated sugar

2 tablespoons chicken stock or water

2 scallions, cut into 2-inch lengths

1 small onion, sliced

1 In a wok or frying pan, heat the oil and fry the garlic until golden brown.

2 Stir in the ginger, then toss in the shrimp. Stirring after each addition, add the pepper, soy sauce, fish sauce, sugar, and stock or water. Stir-fry together for about two minutes, then add the scallions and onion. Stir once, remove from the heat, and turn onto a serving dish.

red color. Add the stock, curry powder, onion, and fish sauce, stirring well after each addition. Thicken with a little of the flour and water paste, adding a little more stock if the mixture becomes too dry. Stir in the scallion and fresh cilantro, and pour the mixture over the noodles.

for the curry

2 tablespoons vegetable oil

2 garlic cloves, finely chopped

1 tablespoon red curry paste (see page 25)

1 cup plus 2 tablespoons coconut milk

1 tablespoon fish sauce

2 teaspoons granulated sugar

3 tablespoons pineapple chunks, cut in half

3 cherry tomatoes, cut in half

6 grapes

20 basil leaves

1 large red chili, sliced

1 Combine all the ingredients for the marinade in a bowl, add the duck, coating it well in the mixture, and let marinate for one hour.

2 Preheat the broiler to a high heat, and broil the duck for five minutes on each side, or until it is seared on the outside but still pink on the inside. Let it cool, then slice diagonally into thin pieces and set aside.

3 In a wok or frying pan, heat the oil and fry the garlic until golden brown. Stir in the curry paste, then add the coconut milk a little at a time—keep stirring—and bring to a boil.

4 Turn the heat down to a gentle simmer and stir in the fish sauce and sugar. Simmer for five minutes, then add the slices of duck.

5 Stir in the pineapple, tomatoes, and grapes, and simmer gently for one minute. Toss in the basil leaves and chili, stir briefly, then transfer to a serving dish.

roast duck curry

gaeng phed ped yang

for the marinade

1 garlic clove, finely chopped

1 teaspoon cilantro root, finely chopped

1/2 teaspoon ground cumin

1 tablespoon fish sauce

1/2 teaspoon granulated sugar

6 ounces duck breast

hot and sour vermicelli salad

yam wun sen

lettuce and parsley, for decoration

1 tablespoon vegetable oil

1 garlic clove, finely chopped

1/4 cup stock, plus extra if necessary

2 tablespoons lemon juice

2 tablespoons fish sauce

1/4 cup lean ground pork

4 large raw shrimp, shelled and de-veined

1/2 teaspoon chili powder

1 teaspoon granulated sugar

6–8 pieces dried mushroom, soaked in water for 20 minutes

4 ounces dry wun sen noodles (see page 24), soaked in water for 20 minutes then drained

2 shallots, finely sliced

1 scallion, chopped

for garnishing

1 sprig of fresh cilantro, coarsely chopped

1 Line a serving dish with lettuce and parsley and set aside.

2 In a small frying pan, heat the oil and fry the garlic until golden brown. Set aside, reserving the oil with the garlic.

3 In a saucepan, heat the stock, lemon juice, and fish sauce, and bring to a boil. Add the ground pork, stirring continuously until cooked through. Add the shrimp and stir, then add the chili powder and sugar. Simmer gently for 15–20 seconds, or until the shrimp are opaque and cooked through. Add a little more stock or water if necessary, to make up to six to eight tablespoons.

4 Stir in the soaked mushroom pieces, noodles, shallots, and scallion, and cook for a few more seconds, stirring constantly, or until the noodles are cooked through and hot. Turn onto the prepared dish and drizzle the reserved garlic oil on top. Garnish with fresh cilantro.

Night stall selling *roti* in front of Wat Mahawan.

baby clams with black bean sauce
hoy pat tow jeow

2 tablespoons vegetable oil

2 garlic cloves, finely chopped

1 pound baby clams in their shells, scrubbed clean

2 tablespoons light soy sauce

1 small red chili, finely chopped

1 teaspoon black bean sauce

1/4 cup water

10 holy basil leaves

1 In a wok or frying pan, heat the oil, add the garlic, and fry until golden brown.

2 Add the baby clams in their shells and stir thoroughly. Add the soy sauce, chili, black bean sauce, and water. Stir thoroughly, then add the basil. Cover with a lid and let the clams steam for a few minutes, shaking the pan occasionally from side to side, until the shells have opened.

3 Discard any clams that have not opened. Give the clams a final stir, to ensure that each one is covered by a little sauce and some chili. Pull off the empty shell tops and discard, then arrange the open clams on a serving dish. Spoon any remaining sauce on top of them and serve.

sausage fried with egg
nam pad kai

In Chiang Mai, this would be made with Ba Yon, raw pork and garlic sausage. Ba Yon (Auntie Yon) was another street vendor whose product became so famous she ended up with her own factory. The northern garlic is so hot you'd think it was chili, and the uniquely round cloves "cook" the raw pork à la Tahitienne. Don't worry—I've simplified this by specifying good old garlic sausage—not as spicy, but tasty nevertheless, and certainly less of a health risk!

2 tablespoons vegetable oil

4 ounces garlic sausage, cut into 1/2-inch slices

2 eggs

2 tablespoons fish sauce

1 whole head fresh garlic or 1 whole head pickled garlic (see page 20),
  peeled and finely sliced

1 large tomato, cut into wedges

3 scallions, coarsely chopped

1 Heat the oil in a wok or frying pan, add the slices of sausage, and stir-fry for a few seconds.

2 Break the eggs into the pan, mix briefly, then add the fish sauce, sliced garlic, tomato, and scallions. Stir-fry over high heat for two to three seconds, then turn onto a serving dish.

pork in chili sauce
nam prik ong

This Chiang Mai dip is sold on the street with bags of deep-fried pork rind—indeed, so much do they go together that there's a popular song about lovers having to be as close as pork and Nam Prik Ong.

2 tablespoons vegetable oil
2 garlic cloves, finely chopped
2 teaspoons red curry paste (see page 25)
1/2 cup ground pork
1 large tomato, finely chopped
2 tablespoons fish sauce
1 tablespoon lemon juice
1 teaspoon granulated sugar

1 Heat the oil in a wok or frying pan, add the garlic, and fry until golden brown.

2 Mix in the red curry paste and cook together briefly. Add the pork, and stir-fry over high heat until the meat loses its pink color.

3 Add the tomato and stir-fry for two to three seconds, then add the fish sauce, lemon juice, and sugar. Stir together for two minutes, then pour into a small bowl. Serve as a dip with raw vegetables.

steamed fish with chili paste
oo pla

In northern Thailand, the street cook would normally wrap this in a banana leaf for steaming—but as the leaves only add flavor when they're broiled, I'm happy to steam this in an ordinary dish.

2 dried long red chilies, seeded and soaked in water to soften
3 garlic cloves, chopped
3 small red shallots, chopped
1-inch piece of galangal (see page 17), coarsely chopped
1 tablespoon chopped lemon grass
1 pound freshwater fish, filleted and cut into 1-inch chunks
2 tablespoons fish sauce
2 basil leaves

1 Using a mortar and pestle, pound together the chilies, garlic, shallots, galangal, and lemon grass to make a paste.

2 Place the fish pieces in a mixing bowl along with the fish sauce, basil leaves, and paste, and mix gently together.

3 Place the mixture in a heatproof bowl and steam for 15 minutes. Serve in the bowl.

2 If using small bananas, cut in half; if using long bananas, cut into three pieces. (You should end up with pieces about 3 inches long.) Cut each piece in half lengthwise to give strips about a half-inch thick.

3 Preheat the oil for deep-frying to 400°F. Dip the banana strips in the batter, shake off any excess, and lower into the hot oil. Fry until golden brown, then remove, drain on paper towels, and serve immediately.

sago and corn pudding
saku khao pohd

(Serves 6–8, see page 14)

2 1/2 cups water
2 teaspoons rosewater
2/3 cup sago or tapioca
1/4 teaspoon salt
1/2 cup granulated sugar
3/4 cup corn kernels, canned or frozen
4 ounces lotus seeds (see page 19)
1/2 cup coconut cream

1 In a medium saucepan, bring the water to a boil. Stir in the rosewater, sago or tapioca, and salt, and cook until the grains have fully swelled and are cooked through—about 15 minutes.

2 Add the sugar and simmer gently, stirring all the time, until the sugar has dissolved. Stir in the corn kernels and lotus seeds.

3 Divide the pudding between six to eight small bowls, top each one with a spoonful of coconut cream, and serve warm.

banana fritters
kruay kaek

A personal favorite, now found all over southeast Asia. I last saw it being made in Lampang market, a banana-growing center near Chiang Mai, where a street cook was deep-frying masses of them in a gigantic wok. For five baht (about 21 cents in 2002) I got an enormous amount, wrapped in a sheet of old newspaper.

1 cup rice flour
1 cup coconut milk
1/2 teaspoon salt
1/4 cup granulated sugar
1 teaspoon white sesame seeds
6 small or 3 large unripe bananas (the skins just turning yellow)
vegetable oil for deep-frying

1 Combine the flour, coconut milk, salt, sugar, and sesame seeds in a bowl, and mix to a smooth batter. Set aside.

Issan, the northeastern province of Thailand, was once considered a punishment post for Thai civil servants. People didn't visit it willingly, and as a result, the region has remained an unspoiled secret for many years. Recently, however, traveling food sellers have introduced special new foods, including grilled chicken and pork, from the northeast to the streets of Bangkok. The region also has many unique religious festivals, including the monk-making ceremony at Ban Ta Klang, in which a procession of brightly decorated elephants traces its way from the river to the temple.

the northeast

spicy beef with dry-fried rice
nua namtok

8 ounces beef tenderloin, about an inch thick

1/4 cup beef stock

2 tablespoons fish sauce

1/4 cup lemon juice

1 teaspoon granulated sugar

1 teaspoon chili powder

2 scallions, finely chopped

2 shallots, finely chopped

1 tablespoon dry-fried rice (see page 29), coarsely pounded

for garnishing

a few fresh cilantro leaves

1 Preheat a moderate-to-hot broiler, and broil the steak for one to two minutes on each side, depending on personal preference. Transfer to a cutting board and slice thinly, retaining any juices.

2 Place the sliced beef and any juices in a saucepan along with the stock, and heat gently. Stir in the lemon juice, sugar, and chili powder.

3 Remove from the heat, stir in the scallions, shallots, and pounded dry-fried rice, and transfer to a serving bowl. Garnish with fresh cilantro, and serve.

beef stewed with noodle
gueyteow nua peui

4 cups beef stock

1 pound lean rump steak, cut into 1/2-inch cubes

3 garlic cloves, roughly chopped

3 cilantro roots

2 cinnamon sticks

4 star anise

2 tablespoons light soy sauce

2 tablespoons fish sauce

1 teaspoon granulated sugar

3 ounces sen mee noodles (see page 24), soaked and drained

2 cups fresh bean sprouts

for garnishing

1 scallion, finely chopped

a few fresh cilantro leaves, roughly chopped

1 Pour the stock into a large pot. Add the beef, garlic, cilantro roots, cinnamon, star anise, soy sauce, fish sauce, and sugar. Bring to a boil and simmer gently for 30 minutes. Skim off the scum occasionally.

2 In the meantime, put the noodles and bean sprouts into a serving bowl. When the beef is cooked, pour the soup over the noodles and bean sprouts, which will cook in the hot stock.

3 Garnish with the chopped scallion and fresh cilantro, and serve.

Sen mee or rice vermicelli noodles.

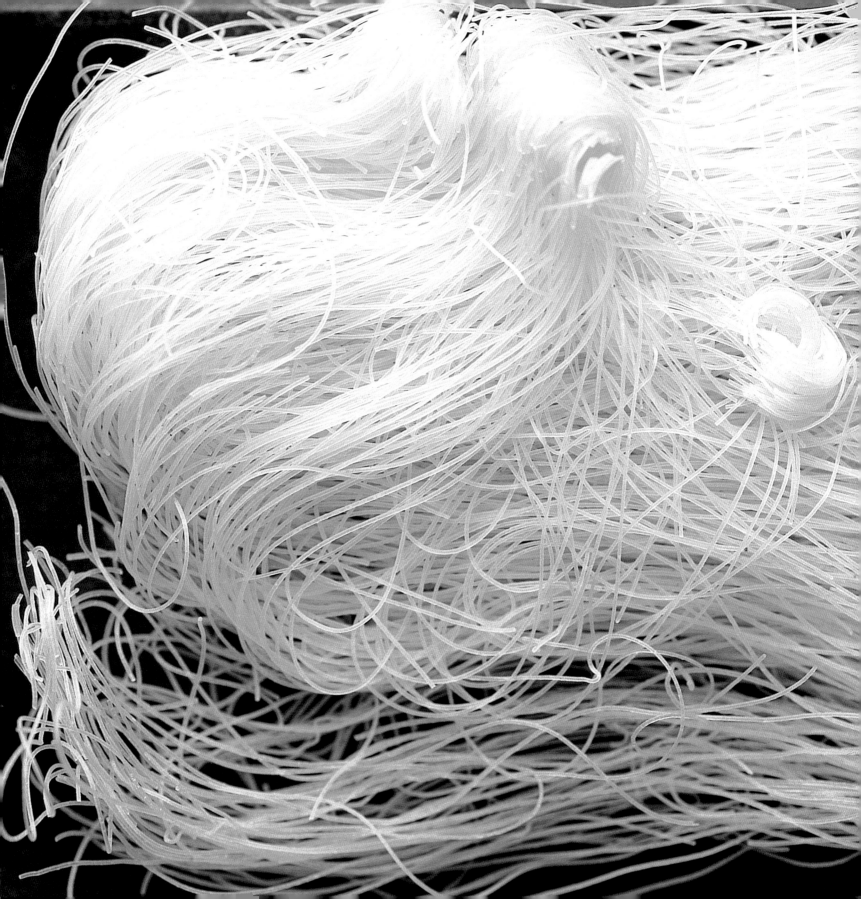

isan sausage si grot issan

Although many types of charcuterie are made in Isan, you see street stalls grilling these sausages everywhere. You buy one on a stick and eat it as you walk along, and if you can balance it, you have a little package of chopped chili, nuts, ginger, and cilantro leaves—a real treat. They are popular among foreign visitors who like the fact that the sausage is freshly grilled and largely untouched by hand.

2 teaspoons finely chopped cilantro root
8 ounces pork belly with fat, ground
3¹/₂ cups boiled fragrant rice
4 ounces garlic (about 2-2¹/₂ bulbs), finely chopped
1 teaspoon salt
about 30 inches of sausage skin

1 Place the ingredients for the sausage filling in a bowl and mix together.

2 Put a funnel into one end of the tube of sausage skin and tie a knot in the other end. Force enough sausage meat into the skin to form a 3-inch length and knead it down to the knotted end. When it is firmly packed, tie a knot in the tube close to the filling. Repeat this process until all the sausage meat is used up—you should end up with a string of five or six sausages. Prick any air bubbles to release the air.

3 Hang the string to dry—you can cook the sausages after one day or you can mature them for up to 48 hours for a "sour" taste.

4 The sausages can either be grilled or broiled (in the entire string or individually), skewered on brochettes, or deep-fried. To test they are cooked, prick them with a fork and if no fat bubbles out when the fork is removed, they are cooked. If you are deep-frying, prick the skin in several places before plunging them into hot oil. Serve with sprigs of fresh cilantro, fine slivers of fresh ginger, ground roasted peanuts, and finely chopped small fresh red or green chilies.

beef curry with bamboo shoots gaeng normai nua

This is another dish always made for temple festivals because it can be produced in quantity. It is offered to everyone: monks, the poor, any passers-by—even gawking tourists. Such acts are tamboon, which means they earn religious merit for those who do them. Appropriately, I last saw it being dished out at the Ban Ta Klang monk-making ceremony when the boys were being shaved and dressed, prior to entering the monastery.

1/2 cup coconut cream

2 tablespoons vegetable oil

1 garlic clove, finely chopped

1 tablespoon red curry paste (see page 25)

2 tablespoons fish sauce

1 teaspoon granulated sugar

6 ounces tender beef steak, finely sliced (about 3/4-1 cup)

1/2 cup beef stock

2 kaffir lime leaves, roughly chopped

3/4 cup bamboo shoots (see page 19), cut into slivers

20 fresh holy basil leaves

1 In a small pan, gently heat the coconut cream but do not let it boil. Cover, and set aside.

2 In a wok or frying pan, heat the oil and fry the garlic until golden brown. Add the curry paste and stir well. Pour in the warmed coconut cream and stir until it begins to reduce and thicken, then add the fish sauce and sugar.

3 Toss the beef into the pan and cook for one minute.

4 Pour in the stock and simmer for a further two minutes, or until the beef is just cooked through. In turn, stir in the lime leaves, bamboo shoots, and basil leaves. Cook gently together for a final minute, then turn onto a serving dish.

broiled chicken with sweet chili sauce gai yang

This used to be a uniquely northeastern specialty, but itinerant street sellers have spread it across the country. Still, as you drive across the invisible border into the province, you know you're in Isan because you begin to see huge, brightly painted model chickens by the roadside indicating the presence of a Gai Yang seller. If you stop, which you should, you'll probably find a clutch of truck drivers perched on small stools, around which live chickens forage for food, impervious to the diners salivating over chunks of golden chicken, grilled on slits of bamboo and served with hot and sweet sauce, and a woven basket of sticky rice—delicious.

for the marinade

2 tablespoons sesame oil

2 garlic cloves, finely chopped

1 teaspoon finely chopped cilantro root

2 small fresh red chilies, finely chopped

2 tablespoons fish sauce

1 teaspoon granulated sugar

14 ounces boneless chicken breasts, with skin

for the hot and sweet sauce

6 tablespoons rice vinegar

1/4 cup granulated sugar

1/2 teaspoon salt

2 garlic cloves, finely chopped

3 small fresh red chilies, finely chopped

1 In a large bowl, mix together all the ingredients for the marinade and let marinate for 30 minutes.

2 Meanwhile, make the hot and sweet sauce. In a small saucepan, heat the vinegar and sugar and stir until dissolved. Add the salt and simmer, stirring, until the liquid thickens. Remove from the heat, pour into a small bowl, and let cool. When the sauce is cold, stir in the chopped garlic and chilies.

3 Preheat the broiler. Broil the marinated chicken for about five minutes on each side, or until cooked through.

4 Arrange the chicken on a platter and serve with the bowl of sauce.

papaya salad som tam

Now the most popular salad in Thailand—you see sellers squatting on the ground, pounding the ingredients everywhere, from garage forecourts to the entrances of grand hotels. There are countless versions, and some highly specialized individual varieties. Even one of the present King's daughters, H.R.H. Princess Mahachakri Sirindhorn, is known for her particular blend, and she has written a popular song about it. I had a small part to play in popularizing the dish when I started my first restaurant in London twenty years ago. Back then, it was commonly thought that Som Tam was too hot for foreigners, but I insisted on putting it on the menu and now it's every-where. If you order one from a street seller, nod or shake your head when the chilies start to go into the mortar, that way you won't end up cooling your head under a faucet. This recipe contains a moderate number, so adjust up or down to taste.

2 garlic cloves, peeled

3–4 small fresh red or green chilies

2 long beans (see page 17) or 5-6 green beans, chopped into 2-inch lengths

6 ounces fresh papaya, cut into fine slivers (about 3/4-1 cup)

1 tomato, cut into wedges

2 tablespoons fish sauce

1 tablespoon granulated sugar

2 tablespoons lime juice

for serving

a selection of fresh firm green vegetables in season—iceberg lettuce, cucumber, green cabbage, and so on

1 Pound the garlic in a large mortar, then add the chilies and pound again. Add the long beans, breaking them up slightly. Now take a spoon and stir in the papaya. Lightly pound together, then stir in the tomato and lightly pound again.

2 Add the fish sauce, sugar, and lime juice, stirring well, then turn into a serving dish. Serve with fresh raw vegetables—any leaves, such as green cabbage, can be used as a scoop for the spicy mixture.

Young green papaya.

skewered marinated pork moo ping

This makes about eight skewers, so have ten available. Try to find six- to eight-inch wooden skewers.

for the pork marinade

2 garlic cloves, finely chopped

6 cilantro roots, finely chopped

1/4 cup fish sauce

1 tablespoon light soy sauce

1/2 cup thick coconut cream

1 tablespoon vegetable oil

1 tablespoon granulated sugar

1/2 teaspoon ground white pepper

1 pound lean pork, thinly sliced into 1 1/2 x 3-inch pieces

for the chili sauce

1 tablespoon fish sauce

2 tablespoons lemon juice

1 tablespoon light soy sauce

1 teaspoon chili powder

1 tablespoon granulated sugar

1 tablespoon coarsely chopped cilantro

1 Combine all the ingredients for the marinade in a bowl and mix well together, making sure that each piece of meat is thoroughly coated. Let marinate for at least 30 minutes.

2 While the meat is marinating, place all the sauce ingredients in a small bowl and mix well. Taste, and if the sauce is too hot, add more fish sauce, lemon juice, and sugar. Set aside.

3 Preheat the broiler. Thread two pieces of meat onto each skewer, making sure that as much of the meat as possible will be exposed to the broiler.

4 Broil over high heat for two to three minutes on each side, or until the meat is thoroughly cooked through. Serve on a dish garnished with lettuce, parsley or cilantro, and with the sauce on the side.

pork toasts kanom bung na moo

Makes about 20 toasts

I last saw this in Surin market, made with long French baguettes, which probably means that the vendor was originally from Cambodia or Laos where they continue to make fresh French bread daily, as in the colonial era. It is best to use slightly stale bread, so it won't soak up too much oil when it's being deep-fried.

5 slices day-old bread
2 garlic cloves, finely chopped
3 cilantro roots, chopped
$^1/_2$ cup ground pork
2 eggs
2 tablespoons fish sauce
a pinch of ground white pepper
1 tablespoon milk or cold water
vegetable oil for deep-frying

for garnishing
cilantro leaves, quartered cucumber, finely sliced rings of red chili

1 Preheat the oven to 250°F. Trim the crusts off the bread and cut each slice into four quarters (or cut into decorative shapes using a cookie cutter). Lay the pieces on a baking sheet and bake in the oven for about 10 minutes, or until the bread starts to crisp. Remove from the oven.

2 Meanwhile, pound the garlic and cilantro roots in a mortar. Transfer to a mixing bowl and combine with the pork, one egg, the fish sauce, and the ground white pepper. Mix thoroughly. Place a scant teaspoon of the mixture on each piece of toast. Combine the remaining egg with the milk or water, and brush lightly over each pork toast.

3 Heat the oil to 400°F. in a deep-fat fryer and fry the toasts, a few at a time, for two to three minutes until golden brown. Drain on paper towels, then arrange on a large plate. Garnish with cilantro leaves, cucumber or chili, or a mixture of all three pierced with a toothpick. Serve with fresh cucumber pickle (Adjahd, see page 25).

jungle curry gaeng pah nua

The most obvious difference between this typical Isan curry and those from further south is that it doesn't use coconut milk or cream, the palm being a coastal plant. They also use particular vegetables, which in the original would probably have been growing wild. And lastly, there's the hot spiciness, which is meant to help "down" large quantities of sticky rice.

2 tablespoons vegetable oil

1 garlic clove, finely chopped

1 tablespoon red curry paste (see page 25)

6 ounces lean beef steak, finely sliced (about 3/4-1 cup)

about 1 cup water

2 tablespoons fish sauce

1/2 teaspoon granulated sugar

10 slivers of krachai (see page 17); if using dried, soak in water for
   10–15 minutes to soften

1-1 1/2 cups prepared vegetables (such as 6 thin green beans, trimmed
   and cut into 1-inch pieces; 1 small carrot, slivered; 2 small green
   eggplants, quartered)

12–15 holy basil leaves

2 whole fresh green peppercorns, or 15 dried black peppercorns

3 lime leaves, finely chopped

1 In a wok or frying pan, heat the oil and fry the garlic until golden brown. Add the curry paste and stir-fry together for five to ten seconds. Add the slices of steak and stir-fry for a further ten seconds. Stir in two tablespoons water, the fish sauce, sugar, and the krachai, cooking for a few seconds more.

2 Toss in the prepared vegetables along with the remaining water, basil leaves, peppercorns, and chopped lime leaves. Stir for a few seconds (just long enough to cook the vegetables, which should retain their crispness).

3 Turn into a bowl and serve.

The author with another greedy elephant.

duck with tamarind sauce ped makarm

6 ounces duck breast

for the marinade

1 garlic clove, finely chopped

1 teaspoon finely chopped cilantro root

1 teaspoon coriander seeds

1 tablespoon fish sauce

1 teaspoon dark soy sauce

for the tamarind sauce

1/4 cup water

2/3 cup palm sugar (see page 20)

3 tablespoons fish sauce

2 tablespoons tamarind water (see page 24)

1/2 teaspoon chili powder

for garnishing

2 tablespoons vegetable oil

3 small shallots, finely sliced

1 Mix all the ingredients for the marinade together in a bowl, add the duck breast, and coat well. Let marinate for one hour.

2 In a small frying pan, heat together the water and palm sugar, stirring constantly. Add the fish sauce, tamarind water, and chili powder, stirring until the sauce thickens slightly. Let cool, then pour into a small bowl and set aside.

3 In a small frying pan, heat the oil and fry the shallots until golden brown. Remove the shallots with a slotted spoon and set aside.

4 Place the marinated duck breast under a hot broiler and broil for four to five minutes on each side.

5 Cut the duck into thin slices and arrange on a serving dish. Pour the sauce over the duck and garnish with the crispy shallots.

sliced steak with hot and sour sauce nua yang

This is very easy to make. In Isan they would probably use water buffalo—and they'd use every morsel, from the intestines to the sexual organs—but here we're going for a simple beef steak.

lettuce, carrot, and cucumber, for decoration

6 ounces lean beef steak
1 tablespoon lemon juice
1 tablespoon fish sauce
1 teaspoon granulated sugar
1/2 teaspoon chili powder
2 shallots, finely sliced
1 small scallion, chopped

for garnishing
1 sprig of fresh cilantro, coarsely chopped

1 Arrange the lettuce, carrot, and cucumber on a serving plate and set aside.

2 Preheat the broiler. When it is really hot, broil the steak so that the meat remains rare on the inside. Slice thinly and set aside.

3 In a bowl, mix together the lemon juice, fish sauce, sugar, and chili powder. Add the shallots, scallion, and slices of cooked beef. Stir quickly, then turn onto the serving dish and garnish with fresh cilantro.

thai dim sum khanom jeeb

Makes 15

This is a Thai version of the classic Chinese dim sum, testimony to the connections between southern China, Laos, and across the Mekong into Isan. The numbers of itinerant Chinese traders and transporters inevitably means enterprising street vendors will try to satisfy their needs by cooking Chinese food, even if the dishes get transformed into distinctly local specialties.

for the wontons

1 cup ground pork

¹/₂ cup shrimp, peeled, de-veined, and finely chopped

3 tablespoons finely chopped water chestnuts (see page 21)

1 tablespoon fish sauce

1 tablespoon light soy sauce

1 tablespoon oyster sauce

¹/₂ teaspoon white pepper

1 teaspoon granulated sugar

15 sheets wonton pastry

for the garlic oil

2 tablespoons vegetable oil

2 large garlic cloves, finely chopped

for the chili sauce

1 tablespoon dark soy sauce

2 tablespoons light soy sauce

2 tablespoons rice or white wine vinegar

2 teaspoons granulated sugar

2 small red chilies, finely chopped

1 scallion, finely chopped

1 Mix the ingredients for the filling together in a bowl and set aside.

2 In a small frying pan, heat the oil and fry the garlic until golden brown. Set aside to infuse, reserving both the oil and the garlic.

3 Make a circle of the thumb and forefinger of one hand. Lay a wonton wrapper over the circle and press the middle to make a little "sack." Place about one tablespoon of the filling inside the "sack," then lightly twist the top edges of the wrapper together to form a loosely closed sack. Repeat to make 15 dim sum.

4 Place the prepared dim sum in a steamer and steam for 10 minutes.

5 Meanwhile, make the chili sauce by combining all the ingredients in a small bowl. Pour the reserved garlic and oil into a separate bowl.

6 Transfer the dim sum to a plate and serve with the chili sauce and garlic oil.

fried catfish with krachai
pad pet pla duk

The Mekong, which forms the frontier between Laos and Isan, also provides plentiful supplies of catfish, which has a flavor quite different from more common sea fish. If you have a good fish market, you could experiment with whatever river fish is available or better still, go fishing yourself.

1 whole catfish, weighing about 10 ounces, or the equivalent available
   freshwater fish, such as trout
vegetable oil for deep-frying, plus 1 tablespoon extra for stir-frying
1 tablespoon red curry paste (see page 25)
1/4 cup coconut cream
2 tablespoons (about 3 small rhizomes) krachai, slivered into
   fine matchsticks
2 tablespoons fish sauce
1 tablespoon granulated sugar
3 kaffir lime leaves, rolled into a cigarette shape and finely sliced
   across at an angle
2 large fresh red chilies, sliced into ovals

1 Clean the fish and pat dry, then cut across into one-inch slices.

2 Heat the oil to 400°F. in a deep-fat fryer.

3 Deep-fry the fish slices until hard but not yet crispy. Drain on paper towels and set aside.

4 In a wok or frying pan, heat one tablespoon of oil, add the red curry paste, and stir well until it begins to blend with the oil—two to three seconds. Add half the coconut cream and stir well, then add the deep-fried fish and coat with the mixture. Stir in the remaining coconut cream, then add the fish sauce, sugar, lime leaves, and chilies, stirring between each addition. Turn onto a dish and serve.

spicy pork noodles with basil leaf
gueyteow pad ki mow

1 tablespoon vegetable oil

1 garlic clove, finely chopped

1–2 small chilies, finely chopped

4 ounces lean pork, thinly sliced

2 tablespoons fish sauce

1/2 teaspoon granulated sugar

10 basil or kaffir lime leaves

1 medium tomato, chopped

8 ounces (wet weight) soaked sen yai noodles (see page 24), rinsed
  and separated

for garnishing

a sprig of fresh cilantro, coarsely chopped

1 In a wok or frying pan, heat the oil and fry the garlic until golden brown. Add the fresh chili and stir for two seconds, then add the pork and stir-fry for a couple more seconds to seal the juices.

2 Add the fish sauce, sugar, and basil or lime leaves, stirring quickly after each addition. Add the tomato, stir until cooked, then add the noodles. Continue to stir-fry over high heat until the pork is cooked through.

3 Turn onto a serving dish and garnish with fresh cilantro. If using lime leaves, you may wish to remove them before serving, since they can be quite tough.

fried egg noodles with tofu
ba mee pad tao hou

2 tablespoons vegetable oil

1 garlic clove, finely chopped

1 egg

1/2 4-ounce cake ready-fried tofu (see page 21), cut into
  1-inch cubes

1 nest egg noodles, dipped in boiling water until just cooked,
  then drained

1 tablespoon preserved turnip (tang chi, see page 20), finely chopped

1 tablespoon light soy sauce

1 teaspoon granulated sugar

1 cup bean sprouts

2 scallions, cut into 1-inch lengths

1 tablespoon crushed roasted peanuts

1/2 teaspoon chili power

1 tablespoon lemon juice

1 Heat the oil in a wok or frying pan, add the garlic, and fry until golden brown.

2 Break the egg into the pan, let set for a moment, then stir.

3 Add the tofu, along with the cooked noodles, and combine well.

4 Stir in the soy sauce, sugar, bean sprouts, scallions, crushed peanuts, chili powder, and lemon juice. Transfer to a serving dish and serve.

Ba mee or egg noodles.

fried vermicelli with pork and scallions pad wun sen

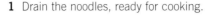

Because these noodles are long, they're always associated with long life. The dish is not chili-hot so it can be eaten by anyone, including little children, which is why you always see it being served up at village festivals like the monk-making celebrations at the elephant village of Ban Ta Klang—of course the wandering elephants are always trying to steal some.

2 ounces wun sen noodles (see page 24), soaked in cold water for
  15 minutes
2 tablespoons vegetable oil
1 garlic clove, finely chopped
4 ounces lean pork, finely sliced
1 tablespoon fish sauce
2 tablespoons light soy sauce
1 egg
2 tablespoons stock or water
1 small onion, slivered
6–8 dried mushrooms, soaked in cold water until soft (about 15 minutes)
  and cut in half if very large
2 scallions, trimmed and cut into 1/2-inch lengths
1/2 teaspoon granulated sugar
ground white pepper, to season

1 Drain the noodles, ready for cooking.

2 In a wok or frying pan, heat the oil and fry the garlic until golden brown. Add the pork and stir-fry briefly until the meat is opaque. Add the fish sauce and one tablespoon soy sauce and stir. Break the egg into the pan and spread it around to cook it a little.

3 Add the drained noodles and mix thoroughly. Add the remaining soy sauce, the stock or water, onion, and mushrooms, and stir quickly to mix well. Toss in the scallions, sugar, and a sprinkling of pepper, stir once more, and turn onto a serving dish.

The author buying food from a *hahp* seller, watched
over by a cut-out portrait of the king.

spring rolls po pea tod

This "Chinese" dish, or more precisely, a Vietnamese/Chinese version of the classic Chinese dish, was probably brought to Thailand by refugees crossing into Isan during the Communist era, many of whom opened restaurants. Actually, I think the Vietnamese food in Thailand is better than in Vietnam itself, since so many restaurateurs were among the small businessmen who were forced to flee. I also think the adaptations to Thai taste improved dishes such as this—but then I would, wouldn't I? However, accompanying any dish with so much fresh salad and vegetables is typically Vietnamese.

for the dipping sauces
1/4 cup granulated sugar
6 tablespoons rice vinegar
1/2 teaspoon salt
1 small red chili, finely chopped
1 small green chili, finely chopped

for the spring rolls
2 tablespoons all-purpose flour
1/4 cup water
6 spring roll sheets (see page 21), 10 inches square
4 ounces wun sen noodles (see page 24), soaked and drained
8 pieces dried black fungus mushroom (see page 17), soaked in cold water to soften and chopped very fine
1/2 cup ground pork
2 garlic cloves, finely chopped
2 tablespoons fish sauce
2 tablespoons light soy sauce
1/2 teaspoon granulated sugar
1/2 teaspoon ground pepper
vegetable oil for deep-frying

1 First make the dipping sauces. Put the sugar and vinegar in a small pan and heat gently, stirring, until the sugar has dissolved. Bring to a boil and boil rapidly until the sauce thickens. Divide between 2 bowls and stir the chopped chilies into one of them.

2 Combine the flour and water in a small saucepan and heat gently, stirring all the time until thick and clear. Pour into a saucer and set aside.

3 Cut each spring roll sheet into four quarters and set aside.

4 Drain the noodles and, using scissors, chop them up into very small pieces. Place in a mixing bowl along with the finely chopped mushroom, ground pork, garlic, fish sauce, soy sauce, sugar, and a shaking of pepper. Combine well.

5 Place the quarters of spring roll wrappers on a work suface and put a heaped teaspoon of the filling on each. Fold in 3 corners to make an envelope shape, and wrap tightly, rolling towards the open corner. Brush a little of the flour and water paste on the open corner and fold it over to seal. At this point, the rolls can be chilled or frozen for future use.

6 To cook, heat the oil to 400°F. in a deep-fat fryer or until a light haze appears. Deep-fry the rolls until golden brown, drain on paper towels, and serve on a plate along with the two dipping sauces.

index

bamboo shoots: beef curry with bamboo shoots 121

bananas: banana fritters 115
· bananas in thick syrup 69
steamed sticky rice with banana 48

beancurd: see tofu
beancurd sheet stuffed with crab 89

bean sprouts: white radish cake with bean sprouts 105

beef: beef and vegetable noodle with black beans 127
beef curry with bamboo shoots 121
beef curry with sweet basil 34
beef stewed with noodle 118
fried marinated beef 126
fried river noodles with beef and dark soy 58
jungle curry 132
sliced steak with hot and sour sauce 135
spicy beef with dry-fried rice 118

bread: puffed bread 77
broiled chili oil 26

cabbage: chicken curry noodle with pickled cabbage 98

chicken: chicken curry noodle with pickled cabbage 98
chicken fried rice with basil leaves 34
chicken rice 55
chicken with curry powder 78
chicken with holy basil 54
curried chicken steamed in banana leaf 65
curried rice and chicken with fresh pickle 67
deep-fried noodles with chicken and mixed vegetables 38
fried noodles with chicken 42
green chicken curry 44
grilled chicken with sweet chili sauce 123
spicy chicken salad 126

chlang mal spicy dip 97

clams: baby clams with black bean sauce 111
clams with chili and basil 91

coconut: baked mung bean and coconut custard 71
coconut custard 70
rice noodles with coconut 54

corn: sago and corn pudding 115
corn cakes 84

crab: beancurd sheet stuffed with crab 89
deep-fried crab claws 79
steamed crabmeat 44

desserts: baked mung bean and coconut custard 71
bananas fritters 115
bananas in thick syrup 69
coconut custard 70
gold threads 69
jackfruit seeds 70
sago and corn pudding 115
steamed sticky rice with banana 48
sticky rice with mango 49
sweet sticky rice balls 22

dry curry paste 26

duck: duck with tamarind sauce 134
roast duck curry 108

eggplants: chlang mal spicy dip 97

eggs: gold threads 69
sausage fried with egg 111

fish: fish cakes with fresh pickle 52
broiled fish with cilantro and garlic 58
fried catfish with krachal 138
fried fish with turmeric 100
pork and fish ball noodles 59
steamed fish with chili paste 112
three-flavored fish 74

fried wonton 39

gold bags 47
gold threads 69
green curry paste 25

hot fire morning glory 42

jackfruit seeds 70

lamb: massaman lamb curry 81

mango: sticky rice with mango 49
massaman paste 26

mung beans: baked mung bean and coconut custard 71

mussels: mussels in batter with egg 60
steamed mussels with lemongrass 75

noodles 24
beef and vegetable noodle with black beans 127
beef stewed with noodle 118
curried noodles 62

deep-fried noodles with chicken and mixed vegetables 38
egg noodles with stir-fried vegetables 102
fried egg noodles with tofu 139
fried noodles with chicken 42
fried river noodles with beef and dark soy 58
fried vermicelli with pork and scallions 140
hot and sour vermicelli salad 110
pork and fish ball noodles 59
rice noodles with coconut 54

spicy pork noodles with basil leaf 139
Thai fried noodles with shrimp 32

papaya salad 124
peanuts: pork fried with chili and nuts 106
pork satay 43

pineapple: fried rice with pineapple 77
pork fried with ginger and pineapple 37

pork: barbecued pork with rice 56
curried pork with pickled garlic 97
deep-fried spareribs 99
fried rice with pork 100
fried vermicelli with pork and scallions 140
gold bags 47
pork and fish ball noodles 59
pork belly with five spices 35
pork fried with chili and nuts 106
pork fried with ginger and pineapple 37
pork fried with red curry paste and long beans 48
pork in chili sauce 112
pork satay 43
pork toasts 131
skewered marinated pork 128
spicy pork noodles with basil leaf 139

red curry paste 25
rice: barbecued pork with rice 56
chicken fried rice with basil leaves 34
chicken rice 55
curried rice and chicken with fresh pickle 67
fried curried rice 101
fried rice with pineapple 77
fried rice with pork 100
fried rice with shrimp and chilies 78
rice soup 47
spicy beef with dry-fried rice 118
steamed sticky rice with banana 48

sticky or glutinous rice 22
sticky rice with mango 49
sweet sticky rice balls 22

sago and corn pudding 115
salad:
hot and sour seafood salad 81
hot and sour vermicelli salad 110
papaya salad 124
southern salad 40
spicy chicken salad 126

sausage: Isan sausage 120
sausage fried with egg 111

seafood: hot and sour seafood salad 81
stir-fried seafood with garlic and peppercorns 87
stir-fried seafood with roast chili paste 92

shrimp: fried shrimp with chilli and lime leaf 63
fried rice with shrimp and chilies 78
hot and sour soup with shrimp and lemongrass 74
shrimp spring rolls 84
shrimp in batter with two sauces 88
shrimp with ginger 107
shrimp with lemongrass 61
shrimp wrapped in beancurd sheet 41
Thai fried noodles with shrimp 32

southern salad 40
spring rolls 141
shrimp spring rolls 84

squid: barbecued squid 87
squid with dry curry 82

taro: fried taro 66
Thai dim sum 136
tofu: fried egg noodles with tofu 139
sweet and sour tofu 92

vegetables: egg noodles with stir-fried vegetables 102

white radish cake with bean sprouts 105